Education for
A Caring Society

WITHDRAWN

WITHDRAWN

Education for
A Caring Society

*Classroom Relationships
And Moral Action*

WITHDRAWN

D. KAY JOHNSTON

FOREWORD BY
JO ANNE PAGANO

TEACHERS
COLLEGE
PRESS

Teachers College
Columbia University
New York and London

24.95

Published by Teachers College Press, 1234 Amsterdam Avenue, New York, NY 10027

Library of Congress Cataloging-in-Publication Data

Johnston, D. Kay.
  Education for a caring society : classroom relationships and moral action /
D. Kay Johnston.
       p. cm.
  Includes bibliographical references and index.
  ISBN-13: 978-0-8077-4718-6 (pbk. : alk. paper)
  ISBN-10: 0-8077-4718-1 (pbk. : alk. paper)
  1. Teacher-student relationships—United States.   2. Education—Moral and ethical aspects—United States.   I. Title.
  LB1033.J64 2006
  370.11'4—dc22

                                                                    2006016520

ISBN-13:   ISBN-10:
978-0-8077-4718-6 (paper)   0-8077-4718-1 (paper)

Printed on acid-free paper
Manufactured in the United States of America

13 12 11 10 09 08 07 06   8 7 6 5 4 3 2 1

This book is for my mother, and in memory of my father.

Contents

Foreword

SOMEONE ONCE SAID that we are born into a world already spoken. We find and form ourselves as members of our cultures through what Clifford Geertz called a "web of significance" woven by language. We become the subjects of the languages we speak. A common language binds us together as members of a community. As Dewey noted, communication and community are related words. Language, and I include here gesture and other modes of expression, is the means by which a relational self is constructed. Schools are a primary agency through which cultural codes are communicated and through which we become members of our communities. This means, as Dewey said, the classroom must become a community. And in a community what is unspoken is as important as what is spoken.

In the current educational climate, what is unspoken is the importance of thinking about relationships in the classroom. There is a good deal of talk about declining morality but little talk of the centrality of relationships to the development of a moral self. Instead, the mainstream conversation about education focuses on individual achievement measured only by standardized test scores. I fear that this focus leads us to think in terms of a selfish individualism and does little to prepare our students to become responsible members of democratic communities.

In this volume, Johnston's major assumption is that all education is moral and political education, and that our failure to speak about this is detrimental to the raising of our children. Her purpose in this book is to enter and continue a "sustained conversation" about the moral imperative to think and speak about relationships in our classrooms. The teachers who participated in this study reveal that this is nearly a taboo subject. They worry that people will think they are "mushy" or "touchy-feely."

We meet some wonderful teachers in this book. When they speak about their practice, their language is one of relationships. And they understand that there are more than two people in the classroom. It is not simply relationships between teachers and individual students that matter but relationships among students as well. At the same time, it is not just about "them"—the students. It is about ourselves as well. We learn from these teachers how important it is for us to reflect on ourselves in relationships. You would be happy to have your children in their classrooms.

As I was reading this book, I found myself thinking about my own teaching. I thought particularly about the first meeting of a new class each semester. The room is tense. Everyone looks straight ahead or down at their desks. No one smiles. They are terrified of one another. And of you too. The most important thing we have to do as teachers is help these individuals become members of a community with a common purpose and a common language. They need to become responsible for one another and for their own learning. Only through striving for community can individual achievement be meaningful.

We want for our students to take their learning personally, to see that what they read and write has implications for the way that they live their lives with others. This is what moral development in the classroom means. For those of us involved in teacher education, we want our students to take their practice personally and to embed that practice in a solid theoretical background. It may not be intuitive to say that this requires the development of trusting relationships. But as Stanley Cavell has noted, there is no alternative to trust in human relationships.

Trust is an issue for Johnston and for the teachers with whom she is in conversation in this book. This issue comes up whether it is in the context of a discussion of cheating or of students' reluctance to ask questions in class. In listening to teachers' conversations, Johnston has been able to map a moral language that enables us to talk about trust in the classroom. Trusting others involves trusting ourselves, something that this book helps us to think about.

No one is questioning the importance of learning to read and write and do math. The claim is that these are empty accomplishments if they do not help us to become better people. This book extends the conversations of such writers as Noddings, Greene, Martin, and Grumet in helping us to think about hard and critical questions.

Jo Anne Pagano

Preface

I HAVE BEEN A teacher for over 35 years, an experience that has consistently challenged and enriched me. This book is a result of thinking about teaching over these years, but more specifically about doing so in a time in which I believe the conversations about teaching and learning are often reductive and troubling. Public conversations about the purpose of education as a vehicle for social justice, for transformation of society, and as a way to learn to think critically have been silenced by the dominant discussion of the purpose of education, framed by economic interests and measured by high-stakes tests.

I have written this book to enter this conversation and, perhaps, to broaden the topic. The goal of education should not be solely focused on developing students who can contribute productively to the economic situation of the society in which they live and who can meet the high standards determined by local, state, and federal mandates. More fundamentally education should be about developing students who can be critical thinkers and participating citizens in an increasingly complex and rapidly changing world.

To contribute in educating this kind of citizen, teachers must attend to the development of students' ability to think of themselves in relationships. This topic has been missing from our public conversations about education even though teachers and researchers in education understand its importance.

Classroom relationships are often thought about in terms of a teacher's relationship with students. Relationships among students are often characterized as peer groups, cliques, and friendships, or described in more negative terms, such as peer pressure, in-groups, and harassment. It is important to look at these issues in a classroom, but classroom relationships mean other things, too. My students tell me that knowing people in class makes a real difference in the way they are able to perform in class. This seems intuitively right—we do better when we trust people to work with us—but how do teachers develop a classroom in which students learn to trust each other? What exactly do we think of as we work to develop this kind of classroom, and why does thinking about it matter?

I have come to believe that developing these types of classrooms requires attending to the relationships that students have with each other and that this, indeed, matters a great deal. How can we work to build a classroom in which relationships become a central focus? One way to sharpen this focus in the work of teaching is to articulate clearly how teachers think about this essentially moral dimension of teaching. We need to be explicit in the way we discuss the importance of relationships in classrooms and the multiple dimensions of these relationships. We also need to think about the connection of these classroom relationships to moral theory and to moral behavior.

In this book, I discuss the reasons that thinking about relationships in classrooms are important and connect those ideas to moral theory. I discuss the idea of classroom relationships with teachers, and outline the ways they think about the many dimensions of these relationships. Their ideas make clear how complicated and often difficult it is in a classroom to develop relationships in which people can speak out and trust one another. These ideas are crucial to consider if we continue to talk about classroom community. I also argue that these ideas are intricately linked to education for social justice.

This book is written for teachers and for those who educate teachers. I write it in the spirit of beginning a conversation with the reader, and my hope is that those who read this book continue the conversation with others who care about these issues.

Acknowledgments

THERE ARE many relationships upon which I have drawn in writing this book. Over the years I have learned from teachers, those who taught me and those with whom I have taught. I owe something to many of them. I wish to acknowledge two of the teachers who have taught me—Carol Gilligan and Nel Noddings. Both of these women have been generous in many ways; I owe them a great deal. I also want to thank the teachers who contributed their time and ideas by agreeing to talk with me: Karen Berg, Russ Duvernoy, Sonja Enstad, Pat McGill, Carol Miller, and Julie Will. They have all contributed to my thinking, not only through the passages quoted in this book, but also through many years of friendship and conversation.

This book has been in the works for some time, and during that time several people have been enormously supportive in specific ways that perhaps they did not even recognize. My thanks to Bill Ayers, Larry Blum, Ulla Grapard, John Hildebidle, Connie Harsh, Margaret Maurer, Barb Miller, Jo Anne Pagano, Abby Rosenberg, and Marilyn Thie. In addition to the support of those already mentioned, I have wonderful friends and a family—aunts, uncles, cousins, nephews, and nieces—upon whom I rely regularly. I especially want to acknowledge my mother, whose support and love never fail, and my brother. Anne Newton, Karen Stahle, Niki Gilsdorf, Heidi Ross, Sarah Wider, Susan Cerasano, and Deborah Knuth-Klenck have also been supportive friends for a long time. There are many other people who matter a great deal to me, and from whom I have learned many things about the joy, responsibility, and complexity of relationships. I am grateful to them all.

The research done for this book was partially supported by grants from The Spencer Foundation and The Colgate Research Council. Tanya Yatsco transcribed interviews for this book. The editors at Teachers College Press have been careful and helpful readers for this work. All of this support has made my work much easier.

Finally, I thank my students. They all keep me thinking about teaching and the moral implications of this hard work. Some of them have become friends, and staying in relationship with them has meant a great deal to me.

ONE

The Limits of Relationships in Classrooms

WHAT DIFFERENCE do the relationships students have with one another make for our teaching? There is no lack of conversation about the importance of the teacher–student relationship. All of us who teach are aware of what a difference—either positive or negative—our connections to our students can make in what we are able to do in our classrooms; but the teacher–student relationship is not the only one that influences how and what our students learn. They are also influenced by their relationships with the other students in the classroom. This is an obvious point and perhaps because it seems so obvious we do not often talk of it, but that relationship, and the potential it holds for students' ethical and cognitive growth, is the focus of this book.

RELATIONAL DILEMMAS IN MY OWN PRACTICE

For some time I have been puzzling over two events that occurred in my teaching. I regularly teach a seminar titled Moral Development and Education. It is a course offered to seniors in the Educational Studies Department and to others who have met the course prerequisites. Several years ago I was presenting a paper at a conference in the middle of the term and decided to give an unproctored midterm on the day I would be away. The results of that decision were painful and long lasting. I won't rehash the details here for I have written about them elsewhere (Johnston, 1991, 1996), but I will explain briefly what happened. A small number of students cheated; they took the opportunity of my being away to bring in notes. We used this cheating incident as a kind of laboratory for our study of morality. The following term, I interviewed most of the members of that seminar. At the beginning of the project I was quite interested to learn whether ideas

1

taken from the moral development literature we were studying influenced their thinking. As my interviewing continued I began to get interested in another issue. I began to think hard about what it means to be in relationship in a classroom. What kinds of relationships do we develop in classrooms and how do those relationships influence our behavior both in and out of class? Does the idea of a classroom community have any connection to these relationships? Do these relationships influence students' behavior and learning?

I began to ask these questions because of what my students told me. As they discussed their response to this cheating incident, they often articulated how upset they were that other students had caused them "to suffer," to be thought of as a potential cheater, or to put them in a position of trying to deal with this dilemma in class. As they spoke of their feelings, no one reported they had spoken to individual students on their own. They chose to feel upset about other students' behavior, but did not see how their own feelings could influence the other students. In other words, they recognized that other students upset them, so the influence of their "friends" was clear, but no students saw how they might influence someone else. They might have chosen not to tell me that they had thought of telling their friends about their concern, but it seemed to me more likely that the possibility of speaking out did not occur to them or, if it did, they rejected the idea. This dilemma in relationship really struck me. I studied moral development in graduate school and was deeply interested in how people think about their relationships. This inability to speak out in a relationship, to say what one actually means, was familiar to me, for in studying with Carol Gilligan, I had learned how women can lose their voice in relationships; however, my students' descriptions of their loss of voice was nevertheless surprising to me. These young adults, male and female, described one another as friends, yet friends could not speak their own mind if it was going to prove difficult. I was puzzled and disturbed by this.

The second puzzling event happened a few years later. I was preparing to present a paper on the topic of the critical question. I had decided to talk about students' questions as a potential turning point in a class. I was thinking about how a genuine question asked by a student could be the moment in a classroom where real thinking began. I asked some of my students to help me think about this question by telling me when they felt comfortable, or when they wanted to ask a question. Frankly, I expected them to say that they ask questions when they know people and feel comfortable. I expected some students to say they didn't always ask questions in big classes, and others to say that nothing stopped them from asking questions—and some students did say those kinds of things. But, in the way students have, they gave me something else to think about. They said things like:

> "I feel pretty nervous asking questions about subjects that I have no prior knowledge of."
> "The only time I feel uncomfortable asking a question is if I don't understand the subject matter and the teacher is the kind who doesn't like people to ask questions on subject matter we should already understand."
> "I ask a question when I feel as if I know whatever the material is well enough to ask an informed question."
> "I ask a question when I'm slightly lost, but not when I'm totally lost" [the question might be stupid].

Other students did not want to waste people's time. Most of the students were not so worried about what the professor would think, unless the professor (like the one described above) did not welcome questions of clarification. They were, however, worried about looking stupid or asking "dumb" questions. I assume that looking stupid was meant in relationship to other members of the class. These are not surprising answers, but what is surprising is that no one said that they were comfortable asking questions when they really wanted to know what other people made of what was being read or said. These students learned that asking questions can function as a way to clarify information or as an indirect statement of competence, but they did not speak about how questions can lead to ideas that are developed in relationship to the text and to others in the class. I was left wondering about the difficulty of inquiry, whether taking a risk to ask a question was indeed difficult for students.

SPEAKING OUT IN CLASSROOMS, SPEAKING OUT IN SOCIETY

These two experiences from my own teaching seemed disparate to me. Yet, as I contemplated them, I was struck with what is similar in them. In both examples there seems to be a lack of trust in relationship. In the cheating incident and in the matter of when to ask questions, fear of speaking out or looking foolish seems embedded in relationship. This fear of speaking out or standing out in relationship is embedded in a classroom. Students are silenced in our classrooms because they don't see themselves in relationship to others, or, if they do, they don't trust those relationships.

I am interested in how we learn to live in a group. How do we learn to be the dissenting voice in a group? How do we learn to be in relationship to someone with whom we are not intimate? What does it mean to think about ourselves as members of a group working together? How do we find a language for these relationships? I have come to believe that these questions are a focus we need to have in all classrooms.

I do not claim my students are representative of every student in every college in the United States. I teach at a private liberal arts university where the majority of the students have had a relatively privileged education. My experience is limited by this context, but I see young people in other contexts, in public schools in which I work, on the streets of the places in which I live and visit, and I talk often to many teachers. Like teachers everywhere, my friends and I talk about what is missing from our professional lives as well as what we still like about teaching. A common observation of teachers from 1st grade to college is that many students do not seem aware of their responsibility to others (see, for example, Pappano, 2004). While we observe this phenomenon in our classrooms, others observe it in the larger world (Bellah, Madsen, Sullivan, Swidler, & Tipton, 1985; Putnam, 2000).

Perhaps there is something missing in the way we deal with one another. I suggest that what is missing may be the explicit acknowledgment that we live in a world together. This world may be the world of a classroom or the bigger world outside of school. There is, however, a connection between the classroom and that bigger world.

THE IMPORTANCE OF CLASSROOM RELATIONSHIPS

This book deals with the importance of classroom relationships. I will explore how teachers think about developing relationships in their classrooms—relationships that a teacher forms with his or her class and with individual students. I also will consider how and even whether teachers think about developing their students' relationships with one another. We need to focus on this explicitly as a goal of education. We need to return to the idea that Dewey and others promoted—schooling is intimately related to how we live our lives. We are in a new century and a different world from that of Dewey. In our world technology allows us to do many things and to access a mind-boggling amount of information (Kegan, 1994). Currently we are required to teach to higher standards and to "reform" education in the way that politicians and state legislatures are pushing us. Yet, as we struggle to incorporate these developments and reforms into public schools, it is crucial to think together about what kind of citizens we are educating and how these citizens may learn to be in relationship to and responsible for one another—others who are known and those Maxine Greene (1988) calls "unknown others" (p. 79). If we lose sight of this goal, we lose the possibility that schools present us to influence our students' development, to teach for social justice, and to truly reform the world in which we live.

My own view is that education is a profoundly moral endeavor. Teaching other people's children is an awesome responsibility (Donaldson, 1978). It is an awesome responsibility because this teaching is not only about content, but also about learning together. Learning together is embedded in the relationships we develop in our classrooms and our schools. Morality is fundamentally a relational issue. Piaget (1932/1965) wrote, "Apart from our relations to other people, there can be no moral necessity" (p. 196). Thus, the moral component of schooling is most fundamental in the relationships we develop with our students and, more important, in those we help them develop with one another. Whether or not teachers consciously think about developing these relationships, their actions in classrooms tell their students a great deal about these relationships. Some people would call this the hidden curriculum—the curriculum that is not taught explicitly in a classroom or school.

It is this teaching about relationships that should become an explicit part of society's conversations about schooling. This aspect of schooling should be part of all teachers' knowledge base, and developing this language and this thinking needs to be part of teacher education both at the pre- and at the inservice levels. Ideas about how people learn to think in more sophisticated and inclusive ways about their responsibilities to others in the world are an important part of education; one place these ideas are articulated is in theories of moral development. Thus, at least some coursework in theories of moral development is not simply one more thing to add to the already overcrowded curriculum for teacher education, but an essential way of learning about the human beings we teach and the human beings we are. In the next chapter I will outline briefly the work of some of the theorists who can help us think about these responsibilities.

TWO

Moral Development:
A Theoretical Perspective

I N THIS chapter I will explain the influences on my thinking about morality and how my own thinking has developed over time. I once constructed these theories as competing claims posited by theorists who were rivals in their thinking; I no longer think in those terms. In some ways, theorists stand on one another's shoulders—that is, we build on what others have done. Others who study moral development do not necessarily use the theories discussed in this chapter in the same way, nor should they; however, my understanding of these theorists informs my ideas of classroom relationships.

JEAN PIAGET

Piaget was interested in how people learned the "rules of the game." The game he ultimately had in mind was that of living in a society, but to study how one learned the rules, he developed an interview method and studied how boys played the game of marbles. *The Moral Judgment of the Child* (1932/1965) is a brilliant book describing both Piaget's method and his findings. He was interested in learning how children developed an understanding of rules. He believed these rules were the foundation for morality and that we learn to respect the "rules of the game" in our society. He also documented that as the boys in his study became older and more sophisticated, they learned that they could change the rules if they all agreed to do so. He was very interested in the negotiation about the rules that preceded the older boys' games.

One of Piaget's main contributions was the development of a way to interview informants—a method of interviewing that he called semiclinical or the interrogatory (1932/1965, 1979). In the interrogatory, the interviewer questioned the interviewee closely about his understanding of the problem to be solved. (I use the word *his* deliberately because all of Piaget's interviews about the game of marbles were conducted with boys.) Piaget wrote that he tried to get to the boys' level of understanding as well as he could. He accomplished this by feigning ignorance of the game and asking questions about each thing each boy said. He never assumed he knew what they meant; instead he asked them. His descriptions of his method are wonderful and worth reading. Especially wonderful are his moments of skepticism about the "truth" of what he was hearing. It doesn't seem he ever thought what the boys told him was the entire truth, but their words gave him a window into their thinking, just as their actions gave him a view of their practice.

Another of his contributions was a description of the difference between the way his informants thought about the game and the way they actually played it. In other words, there was a difference between children's judgment about the rules and their actions in playing the game. This differentiation helps us understand how we can think one thing, but act in another way. For example, all of the students involved in the cheating incident described in Chapter 1 thought that cheating was wrong. Yet, some of them did it anyway.

In his book, Piaget (1932/1965) describes a change in both the way the boys understand the game of marbles and the way they play it. In first thinking about the rules, the boys believe that the rules are inviolate and that they are passed on from fathers to sons. There are wonderful moments when little boys inform him that the rules come from "the gentlemen of the commune or from God" (p. 59). As the boys get older and have more experience with the game, they learn that the group of boys actually playing a game of marbles can decide on the rules of the game. There is much to discuss about this sequence he describes. But for the purposes of this chapter, I will call attention simply to the idea that the boys learn that the rules don't come from an outside authority, but that they can be developed by the boys themselves. Piaget called this discovery the move from heteronymous to autonomous thinking.

The second description Piaget gives us is how the boys actually play the game of marbles. At first it is what he calls a motor game. They simply play with the marbles; they don't actually play a game. Then they learn that the object of the game is to play by the rules and win; yet, even as they believe the rules are written in stone, they cheat. The practice of the game changes as they learn that it is cooperation among peers that contributes to the competition and that they can make up new rules for a game into which they enter.

This is a very simple interpretation of this very important book. Piaget also studied children's thinking about lies, stealing, and the development of the understanding of intention. For me what is significant is the importance of listening to what people say in order to attempt to understand how they make meaning in the world. It is also significant that Piaget studied boys' games and dismissed girls' games as not addressing what he was interested in. He tells us this—and one response to this information is, "Fair enough," but, of course, one also must consider what he missed by dismissing girls' games. I will return to this point later when I write about Gilligan's work and her attention to "discrepant data."

I cannot discuss Piaget's work without thinking about the implications of a stage theory. He wanted an orderly progression of development. That is what he describes in *The Moral Judgment of the Child*; he writes of a series of more nuanced and sophisticated ways of understanding how to play marbles. There is much justified criticism of stage theories now, some 70 years after he wrote that book. I count myself among the many who disagree with a set progression of steps through which we all, regardless of specific combinations of sex, race, class, culture, sexual orientation, and other differences, move. The theory of a universal pattern of development and an ideal of a highest stage, one that is obviously best, is not compelling in a postmodern world. I do, however, want to hold on to the idea that we do change in the way we understand the world and make meaning in our lives, and that those changes can be judged, albeit tentatively, as better or worse as we learn the rules of the game, or, to put it more comfortably for me, as we learn to live together in an increasingly complex world. Our experiences inform this change, and it is the experience of education that holds the promise and the possibility of learning to be more responsible in our relationships. This learning about relationship then holds the promise of learning to become more responsible citizens, a point I will discuss later.

LAWRENCE KOHLBERG

Piaget's work on moral development was not picked up immediately in the United States. In fact, to my knowledge Kohlberg was one of the first people to build on it. Again, there are many books describing in detail

Kohlberg's contributions to the field of moral psychology. As with Piaget, I will not attempt to summarize Kohlberg's work except as I see it building on Piaget's and then leading to the work I did myself.

Kohlberg (Kohlberg, 1969, 1976; Kohlberg, Levine, & Hewer, 1984) used Piaget's ideas of both stage theory and methodology as he developed his theory of moral development. His question, like all theorists' questions, was contextualized in his time. He was passionate to know how people learn to discern and disobey immoral authority. This question, coming from his experience as a Jew during World War II, is a profound one (Kohlberg, 1948). It is my belief that the power of this question provides both the importance of and the difficulty with Kohlberg's theory.

Kohlberg, like Piaget, used semiclinical interviews to develop his theory. His initial sample was 60 men, and while he later interviewed both men and women, the women tended to score at a lower stage than the men. From the interviews, he developed a stage theory about the way people understand the idea of justice. There originally were six stages in his theory, and at each stage a person took more information into account as, like Piaget's boys, they understood morality to be located in themselves rather than coming from some outside authority. As I indicated above, few people today find rigid stage theories that seem to proclaim a grand truth convincing. While I am not persuaded by stage theories, I am interested in the way Kohlberg described changes in how people learn to think about morality. Kohlberg believed that educators can and should move students to higher stages of moral reasoning. I don't think that stage change in and of itself should be an educational goal. I am persuaded, however, that, as Kohlberg and Mayer (1981) describe, changes in thinking can be facilitated by conversation, especially conversation with adults or others who can think about issues with more experience. This is the kind of conversation and thinking that Lev Vygotsky (1978) points to in his ideas about the zone of proximal development. So one of the ideas I take from Kohlberg is that we can learn to think in better, more complicated ways about the moral problems we face as human beings.

Another contribution Kohlberg's work makes to my thinking about this issue is the idea of justice upon which he built his theory. Again, I refer you to his work for a full explanation of what he meant by this, but he put great weight on the ability to think impartially and to use justice criteria to solve problems. He was influenced by Rawls in his ideas about impartiality (see, for example, Rawls, 1999). He wrote that we should make moral decisions without concern for the specific individuals involved. In other words, we should make decisions that would be fair to anyone involved in the problem. He also believed that to avoid making decisions based only on what we need or want, we had to apply a universal standard to our decision making. Therefore, anyone facing the same problem would agree that the decision was the right one because it was just to all concerned.

As I think about the question that I believe guided Kohlberg's work, I understand how important these ideas are. That is one of the evolutions in my own thinking. At first I saw his ideas as opposed to those that Gilligan, discussed next, proposed. As I did my own work, I began to understand them as alternatives. I also began to understand that there is a power in believing that something can be universal, that something could be deemed right no matter where you are or who you are. I understand the seductiveness of that idea, even though I find myself in a place that ultimately doesn't believe that universalism is possible, and I find myself saying too often, "It depends."

CAROL GILLIGAN

As many people know, Gilligan began her work interested in the connection between how one thinks about a moral problem and how one acts. I think it is important to understand that she did not set out to study women. Her decision to study women who were making a decision about abortion was the result of her intended study of Vietnam draft resisters being rendered moot by Nixon's abolishing the draft (Gilligan, 2000). So she turned to the study of another problem that our society would deem moral—a study of the decision whether to terminate a pregnancy.

Gilligan, like Piaget and Kohlberg, used semiclinical interviews in her study. She was interested in how individual women thought about their decisions about abortion. While listening to these women talk, Gilligan heard concerns about responsibility in relationship. Rather than ascribing this "relational voice" to Stage 3, as Kohlberg had done in his scoring of the Heinz dilemma, or ignoring what could be called discrepant data, as Piaget had done, she listened to that voice and came to understand that it was a distinct view of moral situations. This voice was concerned with issues of relationship and how to take care of everyone affected by the dilemma. Sometimes the care voice included caring for the "self"—the person who presented the dilemma—and sometimes it did not. Gilligan developed a theory that posited a moral voice of care and a self that was connected to others. She documented her findings in 1977, and in 1982 the publication of her book *In a Different Voice* started a kind of "war" among moral development scholars. I use the word *war* purposefully, because the energies of many people in the field of moral development became consumed by debating which theorist—Kohlberg or Gilligan—was right, who had the truth? Two of the major battles in this war were about gender differences and whether the ethic of care really counted as moral thinking.

MY WORK

This is the point where my own work began. I was interested in knowing how people thought about issues of what have been called justice and care in discussing moral dilemmas.

The Fable Study

When I began my graduate work I was working in public schools as a reading specialist and was a reading director. Because I was interested in reading and especially reading comprehension, I wondered whether these moral ideas could be noticed in children's comprehension of reading material. In a small study, I used a semiclinical interview modeled after Piaget's methodology to ask children about the dilemmas embedded in two of Aesop's fables, specifically, "The Dog in the Manger" and "The Porcupine and the Moles."

I omitted the morals attributed to Aesop and asked the children what the problem was and how they would solve the dilemmas in the fables. The children used words like *responsibility* and *care*, as well as discussing rules and ideas about fairness, to describe what they thought the lessons in these fables were. Both boys and girls saw different morals or lessons in these fables, and their thoughts echoed the theories of Kohlberg and Gilligan not only in their ideas about what the dilemma was but also in their ideas about how to solve it. For example, they would solve the dilemma of a porcupine becoming an unwelcome guest in the moles' cave by saying, "A rule is a rule, so the porcupine has to leave the moles' house." Or they would say, "The moles made a promise so the porcupine has to stay." These solutions clearly are based on rules of fairness and issues of justice. Other children would say that they should all move to a bigger cave or "wrap the porcupine in a towel." These kinds of ideas clearly would appeal to someone who wanted to keep the animals in a relationship or who thought that there was a relationship that shouldn't be disrupted. After I had exhausted the ideas that a child had, some would tell me they couldn't think of any other way to solve the problem. They might tell me something like, "Well, that is just the way it is." However, some children would say something like, "Well, we will just have to shoot the porcupine," or "We will have to blow up the cave" [in which the moles and the porcupines live]. I was puzzled by these answers and they stayed with me as unanswered questions. Why did some children, mostly, but not only, boys, think about a solution that seemed violent, when I pushed them as far as they could go with the problem? The study provided a window into the way that these theories actually worked in the ideas of children and a clear connection of moral thinking to what could be considered more traditional reading comprehension work.

At about the same time as I was beginning to use the fables, others were working on learning to hear these moral orientations or voices in real-life dilemmas told in interviews conducted by the Gilligan research group. Lyons (1983) developed a coding scheme and differentiated two orientations in interviews about real-life moral dilemmas. She defined the moral orientation of rights as understanding that moral problems are "issues/decisions of conflicting claims between self and others (including society). These issues are resolved by invoking impartial rules, principles, or standards which consider one's obligation, duty, or commitment; or standards, rules, or principles for self, others and society." The moral orientation of care or response focuses on moral problems as issues of how to respond to others in their situations. In order to do so, one considers how to "maintain relationships" or "promote the welfare of others or prevent them harm or relieve their burdens, hurt, or suffering, physical or psychological" (p. 134).

I relied on that logic and built on that scheme in my own work. Eventually I developed a method of interviewing using the fables (Johnston, 1988). I used the same fables I had used in the preliminary study previously described, and developed a set of questions that I asked each person who agreed to talk with me. The unique contribution my work made was not to assume that a person's first answer is the only idea that individual has about the situation. While the adolescents were able to discuss both moral orientations previously described, when asked which provided the better solution to the dilemma, they chose one orientation as the better solution. Mine was not the only study to demonstrate that both males and females used both moral orientations (Gilligan & Attanucci, 1988; Lyons, 1983), but mine was the first to systematically examine that issue.

I am convinced that most of us use ideas found in both the moral orientation of justice and that of care in solving our moral problems. I also believe that one of those orientations usually seems to provide the better solution to a given dilemma. I think the decision of which seems better is related to gender differences and to the context of the dilemma (Johnston, 1985; Johnston, Brown, & Chrisopherson, 1990; Langdale, 1983). It seems like a waste of time to argue that these differences are either essentially related to gender or nonexistent (Lifton, 1985; Walker, 1984).

Using Both Justice and Care as Ways to Think About Moral Problems

For me, the central issue about these orientations is how we teach children to use both to solve moral problems. It is a central concern because they provide alternative ways to think about moral problems and to conceptualize the moral problem solver in relationships to others in the dilemma. I do not believe one of these orientations is concerned about relationships and the other about some abstract principle. Instead, both orientations can be used to make decisions about how one behaves in a moral dilemma and in the relationships, both intimate and distant, in which most dilemmas are embedded.

In thinking through the dilemma using the questions that come from a justice orientation and the questions that come from a care orientation, one might find alternative ways to think about the dilemma, and that might lead to a good solution. The difference may be in the view that the perspective of justice and the perspective of care give to both the moral dilemma and the relationships involved. The angle is different. One way to think about these alternatives is to imagine them as capturing different aspects of a dilemma. Gilligan (1988) compares this with thinking about ambiguous figures. In one example of an ambiguous figure, if you look at it one way you see an older woman; in another way, you see a young woman. Another ambiguous figure is the vase and the face, and yet another is the rabbit and the duck. If you think about the way you look at these figures, one way allows you to see some aspect of the figure; another way allows you to see another perspective. These orientations work in the same way; switching orientations may let you see a moral problem in a different way. It may provide an alternative way to look at things.

Gilligan demonstrated the problems that occur when women think that the only way to solve a moral problem is to think about how to care for others and not care for oneself. These women lost sight of themselves. She wrote extensively about this problem and demonstrated the importance of women learning to include themselves in those they care for. In other words, some women need to learn how to see moral problems from a justice perspective and treat themselves justly. Some men need to learn to do this, too.

On the other hand, if a person looks at things only from the justice orientation, she or he may run the risk of not attending to others in the dilemma. The person might think that she or he can walk a mile in another's shoes and figure out what everyone else thinks without really knowing the other perspectives in the dilemma.

And perhaps having only one way to look at a moral problem might become frustrating, if that one way does not provide a satisfactory solution to the problem. I mentioned earlier a lingering question from early work using the fables—the children who became so frustrated with trying to think of various ways to solve these dilemmas that they said, "Well, we will just have to shoot the porcupine." This hypothetical violence, this frustration, may be the result of a person's inability to think of another alternative to a situation. I continue to think about this as I do this current work and will return to this topic in Chapter 6.

The frustration that may result in a lack of moral alternatives is speculation, but it is certain that both of these orientations can lead to dead ends in our thinking and knowing the logic of both orientations can provide the problem solver with a different way to see/solve a moral dilemma.

Justice and Care Provide Different Perspectives

One example of how these orientations can provide alternatives for moral problem solving is demonstrated in an interview I did with a seventh grader (in Garrod, 1992). She was asked whether she had ever been in a situation that was unfair. She said she didn't know how to approach a teacher in whose class she was lost. We followed the protocol for that interview question and got to the next question, which was about someone not listening. This interview protocol was designed so that one question used the word *fair* to elicit ideas about the moral orientation of justice, and the moral orientation of care was connected to a question about someone not listening. While answering the question about listening, she returned to the issue of the class in which she found herself lost; however, this time in constructing the problem as someone not listening, she understood that she had to speak in order to be listened to. In other words, it wasn't simply a question of unfairness on the teacher's part that she was lost—her construction of the problem using one perspective. When she thought about the problem from the care perspective, she saw that she wasn't holding up her part of the relationship. Talking through this problem using both ideas allowed her to find a solution, which she would not have found thinking only in one way. Thus, the two orientations make a person ask different questions about a problem.

In *The Nature of the Child* Jerome Kagan (1984) argues that we should instruct children to solve problems by thinking through alternatives and then deciding which of several alternatives provide the best solution to the dilemma. He argues this for all kinds of problems. One of the problems that we all face is determining the right thing to do in a given situation. It seems clear that the two orientations described in this chapter can provide alternative ways to think through a moral problem. When we think through the problem using a care orientation, some issues become salient; when we use the justice orientation, other issues present themselves. As an individual thinks through a problem with these alternative orientations, different aspects of a solution or, in fact, different solutions may present themselves. For me this is the significance of these orientations, not that one is linked to women and the other to men, although there may be a tendency for that to occur. If both men and women think through moral problems using the logic of both orientations, both men and women may be better able to decide on solutions to dilemmas they face.

Both of these orientations provide a way to look at moral problems and to think of the self in relationship. The view of the self in relationship may be different in each of these orientations, but the focus remains on relationships in which a person is embedded. It is to the topic of relationship that we turn in the next chapter.

THREE

Doing Right by Them:
The Relational Landscape of Classrooms

I N A CLASSROOM, a teacher would acknowledge being in relationship with the students; at the very least, most teachers would say that having reasonably good interactions with students results in a better feeling in the classroom. Relationships, however, are involved in more than classroom interactions—learning is embedded in relationship. Relationships affect students not only in how they think and act, but also in what kinds of intellectual risks and ethical stands they take. I came to understand this in a more profound way as a result of interviewing the students described in Chapter 1. I have always known that relationships in the classroom are very powerful for students, but before I began to listen to my students talk about cheating and asking questions, I don't think I realized with such clarity how influential these relationships are. I believe classroom relationships are the ground on which students think and act—the ground on which students learn both cognitive and ethical habits of mind. The ability to speak out, and possibly seem different or articulate a different view, is linked to the trust that students have in the teacher and in one another. Of course we know this, but I don't think we talk enough about it. We are not explicit that the power of relationships is connected to both good and bad outcomes in the classroom, and I don't believe we attend enough to the relational dynamics of the classroom. We think about bullying, about harassment, and about discipline, but those ideas often are not placed in a relational context. I think there is a consequence to this silenced aspect of teaching. When I spoke with teachers, they talked with great conviction about the relationships in their class, yet even as they spoke about this, they acknowledged that it was often something dismissed in conversations about teaching. I will return to this point at the end of this chapter, but first it is important to understand how classroom relationships can be described.

THE INTERVIEWEES

When I began to think about this, I wondered how other teachers think about these issues. I decided to talk with the six teachers whose ideas have contributed to this book. They are not "representative" of teachers everywhere or even somewhere in particular. They are not ethnically or racially different and they are all about the same age. The only real difference is geographic, and even that isn't much—New York and Massachusetts. I chose them to talk with because I know them well. Three of them have supervised my student teachers since 1987, and I worked with the others in public school in Massachusetts, so I have known them for over 30 years. I chose them because I have a relationship with each of them and in that relationship we have had sustained conversations (Hollingsworth, 1994) about teaching. As you read their words, you may find their ideas to be like your own, or yours may be very different. That is, however, exactly what I hope happens. My purpose is to make explicit our relational reflections on teaching and to begin a conversation with you, the reader, about how their thoughts are like and not like your own.

The teachers who participated in this study agreed to talk with me when I first asked them. It seems banal to say, but all of us want to talk about our work as teachers and often are not given that opportunity. I talked with each teacher individually. In each conversation, I wanted to follow certain ideas: I wondered what they defined as the moral dimensions of their classroom and what kinds of student interactions they hoped to foster. I also wanted to know whether these interactions seemed to be a part of the moral dimensions of their classrooms. I was interested in following the ideas they had about developing a self in community and an achieving self in their students. In order to follow these ideas, I developed a protocol of guiding questions that I asked each of them, but each of our conversations took its own course. The following questions were used as starting points for conversations and were adapted from Gilligan, Langdale, Lyons, and Murphy (1982) and Brown and colleagues (1987).

- Can you describe yourself as a teacher?
- How have you changed?
- If you think about teaching, can you describe a moral conflict that you have had in the classroom?
- What would your ideal kind of classroom interaction be?

- When you think about the relationships you want students to have in your classroom, how would you describe them? Is that a moral consideration for you?

I have given pseudonyms to all of the teachers; two of those pseudonyms, Chris and Lesley, are gender neutral. In all cases, I have used the pronoun *she* or *her* to refer to the teacher, so that the one man I talked with will not be identifiable.

In this chapter I will illustrate the relationships that these teachers described as they talked about their teaching. In the next chapter I will map the dimensions of these relationships through the language used to describe them.

THE INTERVIEWS

I began by asking each teacher to describe herself as a teacher. It may seem odd to begin to discuss teachers' answers to this question in a chapter about relationship, but in answering this question, every teacher described herself in relationship to the students in her classroom. They described themselves as people embedded in relationships, and these self-descriptions linked to the ideas that Gilligan (1982) articulated and that were described in Chapter 2.

Relationships to Students

Lesley began by saying, "I am caring and involved." This caring is demonstrated by her behavior with the children. She is always watching and listening to the students and asks a lot of questions, not only of them, but also of their parents. "I want to know what they are thinking and I want my room to be cozy." Lesley wants the room to be cozy because the children need to be "comfortable working and learning there; I don't think stress is good for the kids in my room." She does not worry that she cannot accomplish what she wants to quickly: "I'm also not afraid to never get there because I don't believe that ever getting there is possible." For Lesley, getting there means "to finish being educated." If she does her teaching well, her students will never finish being educated. So in her first words about herself as a teacher, she describes the atmosphere she wants in order for her students to "begin to get there." She believes in the importance of being comfortable in order to take the risk of learning.

In describing herself, she says she has an "educational faith that what we are doing is important." She also speaks about the fact that while she must believe that she might be a child's last chance, she also must believe she won't be. In her self-description she points to an obvious but important aspect of teaching: We know we are not the only teacher our students will have. For some of our students we will be the teacher who makes a difference; for others we won't. This fact makes us vulnerable in our classrooms; our relationships won't always be positive. This fact also puts teachers in relationship with one another. Teachers have to take responsibility for their students' learning and development seriously, and at the same time understand that what they do has been influenced by the teachers who have preceded them and will influence those who will follow them. Teaching is a relational activity both with students and with their other teachers.

May looks at each of her students as an individual and describes how she is always watching and listening to them. She describes herself as a "kid-watcher." She is more confident in herself as a teacher now than she used to be, and not "so reliant on what everybody else wants me to be doing." Yet at the same time she "cares an awful lot about what people think of me as a teacher." May, like Lesley, begins her self description in relation to her students. Note also how they use the same language to describe their work—they both watch and listen to their students. These activities of watching and listening are relational activities. Watching others and listening to them help us understand them. Of course, teachers watch and listen to understand students' learning, but they also learn about the individual students by paying attention to them in this way. Like Lesley, May understands that the work of teaching is always unfinished; however, May also points out another important aspect of the work of teaching—it is always judged by others.

All four of the other teachers with whom I talked also described themselves as a teacher in relationship to their students. Emily said, "It is important to me to be fair," which for her means "giving everyone a chance to tell me what they think." At the end of the year, Emily asked the children to give her a report card; she reported that the kids gave her an A+ on being fair. This was the first thing she said in her self-description. We will return to the word *fair* in the next chapter.

Molly describes herself in lots of different ways, but says that she has high expectations for kids and wants to make some personal connection with kids. She tries to teach kids to make choices. Chris says she is not very structured, but she feels she has a gift for working with kids to do the right things. She said, "I create something, I paint something that the kids can relate to."

Mary wants to develop independence in her students. She also says she feels like a mother sometimes because "she talks to her kids [students] the same way she talks to her kids at home and that's the feeling that is there." Her words echo the work done by others (Grumet, 1988; Ruddick, 1989) who have explored the nature of teaching by comparing it with mothering. In the past I found that argument was not very convincing; after all, not all teachers are mothers and I thought that making that comparison excluded the feelings of many teachers. As I think about it in connection to the subject of this book, I am inclined to rethink my initial reaction. The relationship of mother to child is one that we understand as deeply loving and responsible. Because we are not used to thinking of ourselves in relationships that are not intimate, we don't have many words to describe the responsibilities we feel in those nonintimate relationships. It may be that the only language available to us when we feel loving and responsible is the language of intimate relationships.

The Limits of the School Year

Mary also said she never has enough time. Both Lesley and May also said that there is not enough time. Teachers know that the relationships they have with students are not likely to be long lasting. The school year has an arbitrary beginning and ending. It is not uncommon for teachers and students to feel a bit sad at the ending of a school year, for it is often a farewell. However, we seldom discuss the limits of this bureaucratic time frame, as these limits structure school relationships. The school year starts and stops according to a calendar. The school day stops and starts according to a clock and is interrupted many times. The school day often is structured in small chunks, so time is always a factor in lessons taught and plans not quite finished. This incompleteness, this "unfinishedness," is the reality of teaching. It contributes to teachers always knowing there is more to do and it contributes to the fact that teachers don't always know whether what they do matters. Philip Jackson (1992) calls this the untaught lesson. We don't know when what we teach will connect with a particular student.

Yet in the midst of these artificial beginnings and endings, of the incomplete knowing that is part and parcel of teaching, these teachers describe themselves in connection to their students. They might have described themselves without reference to their students, they might have talked about how they interact with the children, or only about what they expect academically of them, but they all described themselves in connection to their students. This speaks to the relationships teachers develop with their students. There is great power in those connections, even if they last for only 10 months; these teachers' words attest to this importance.

Change over Time

There is one more point to be made about the self-descriptions that these teachers offered. They have all taught for at least 15 years, so I was curious about whether the way they thought about themselves had changed from the way they thought when they began. In thinking about this question, all of them said they had changed, and again they described the changes in relational terms. They described changes in their relationships with their students and with their colleagues.

Lesley and May both say they are more confident. Lesley says she is not as "democratic," she doesn't negotiate as much with her students. She has more confidence in the work she expects them to do. Emily said she takes more risks. She is also more explicit about what she wants the children to do. Mary, too, has become surer of her decisions, especially about things like when to give kids extra chances. Molly has become less rigid and more patient, but more careful about how she extends herself to people. All of these changes have come from the specific experiences of these teachers. Teaching has given them more confidence in their work with children and more confidence in their own voice in the classroom.

One of the questions often asked in connection with relationships is, "In whose terms is the relationship defined?" (Gilligan, 1982; Gilligan, Ward, & Taylor, 1988). Asking this question makes it clear that a relationship is not dictated by the desires of only one person in the relationship. All involved must have a voice in the relationship. Voice is not simply a metaphor; it literally means that those involved in the relationship make a difference in the direction the relationship is taking. These teachers are not simply serving their students; they care deeply about what happens in their classroom, but they also have confidence in their abilities and judgments in their classroom. While they might worry about the balance of their voice and those of their students, they are truly present in their classroom and in relationship with their students. Worrying about the balance of their own voice and those of others presents moral dilemmas in schools, and we turn next to those.

MORAL CONFLICTS IN THE CLASSROOM

In order to understand how each of these teachers understood the moral realm in her work, I asked each to describe a moral conflict that she had faced. I have not used the teachers' pseudonyms in describing the following dilemmas. All of these dilemmas involve people with whom they work, and even if people's names are changed, issues of confidentiality occur. Identifying who said what doesn't seem important. Here again the power of relationship in schools is demonstrated—all the conflicts described by these teachers are embedded in relationships. Some characterized these conflicts in terms of fairness, and others as issues of connection. I first will describe the moral conflicts and then explore how these conflicts are rooted in relationships.

Valuing Every Student

Two teachers described moral conflicts that revolved around treating everyone fairly. One worries about gender equity, and another about heterogeneous grouping—specifically about how to treat the brightest kids in the room. The teacher who worries about gender equity said it is always in the back of her mind, but as she reads and hears more and more about it, she understands more about what she needs to do. She works on it because it is "the fair thing." It is fair because if you treat different kinds of children differently, the children "are not going to see themselves as important." This dilemma of fairness is significant because being fair involves treating both boys and girls with equal attention so that each child recognizes his or her importance in the teacher's eyes. This adds an important dimension to the way we typically think of fairness. Treating people fairly is not simply an issue of equity; it also entails giving each child a feeling of self-worth that results from another person treating one with fairness. This should not be confused with the idea of simply developing the self-esteem of a student; the feeling of being valued in relationship is not only about how students feel about themselves, but about how they see themselves reflected in the relationships in which they learn and grow.

Another teacher talked about issues of fairness in relation to grouping. This person said, "We are directly responsible for whether that child is going to have the background to succeed when he or she leaves school," and worried that possibly the brighter kids could be challenged more. Fairness plays out differently in these two conflicts, but in both conflicts it is directly related to the responsibility and relationships that teachers have with their students.

Teaching What Is Important

Without any hesitation, another said achievement tests present a moral conflict for her. She feels it is very important to teach them certain things and not important to teach them things that are going to "be on the test"; however, the children will be judged by those tests so she must adjust what she wants to teach. The conflict in doing both is time. Many teachers described not having enough time to teach everything that they think is important and that tests and other educational stakeholders (Connelly & Clandinin, 1988) require of them. One of them put it this way: "You have to make choices about what is important to teach." When I asked what is at stake in this moral conflict, she replied, "Doing right by them" and "Doing things I don't believe in." When she feels it is necessary to make choices, like preparing students for a test, something she doesn't believe in, she said, "I am not really myself." This "not being myself" is a moral conflict and it affects not only her sense of self, but also her relationship with her students.

This feeling of being untrue to what they would like to do in a classroom is one with which I think many teachers struggle. One of the teachers in this study said, "I feel like I am copping out" when I don't do all that is required of me. By all that is required of her, she means doing what she fundamentally knows is good teaching in addition to teaching what will prepare students to pass high-stakes tests.

On a day that I was observing in a school, I ran into a teacher who told me she was preparing to retire early. Although she had a wonderful reputation with parents, students, and other teachers in the school, she was leaving teaching at the end of that school year. Her comments and the anguish with which she spoke to me relate directly to the moral conflicts described above. She told me that everything we, meaning educational professionals, have learned in the past that we know is good for children, we have had to abandon in favor of preparing children to meet the standards set by those who aren't in our classrooms. Perhaps we have not had to abandon "everything," but the reality of this problem should not be underestimated. This conflict should not be taken as a simple desire to have no tests, or to have no outside influence in a classroom, but should be looked at as a real conflict of curriculum embedded in the relationships teachers have with their students. It is important to "do right by them."

Public conversations about state-mandated higher standards often characterize teachers and other educational professionals as against standards, as if a simple dichotomy for or against them captures our thinking. Teachers are portrayed as against tests and state standards because they don't want to work hard, or because the teachers themselves could not pass the required tests. In other portrayals, standards become the opposite of some kind of touchy-feely teaching. In fact, the teachers in this study who are concerned with their connections to children also have high expectations for students. It is not an either–or proposition. The conflict is that these teachers know that they believe in and can teach in a way that has been identified as teaching for thinking and real learning, but this kind of teaching must be replaced by teaching that is simply a transfer of information so that their students can meet state-mandated requirements. This is not a problem of teachers being afraid to work; it is a moral conflict because teachers want to do what is right for their students, and for many teachers, what they are "required" to teach makes them leave out many other important topics.

Resolving Issues with Parents

Another teacher described two different conflicts with parents. Both conflicts occurred when a parent objected to aspects of the curriculum in her classroom. In one, a parent had misunderstood her. She was doing what "was perceived [by that parent] as something else." In the second, parents disagreed with something she taught. The similarity in both of her conflicts was the importance for her of talking with the parents about the issues. She wanted to do the right thing in terms of her responsibility to the parents, yet not abandon what she believed was essential in her curriculum. As she described thinking about this, she said, "At that point one part of me wanted to argue with him about those issues and another part of me said that's not what I'm here to do. That's not the issue for us—to see whose belief, you know, wins." She began to feel that the right thing in this dilemma "gets people to the state of everybody being happy." In order to do that, she had to do a lot of talking with one of the parents and she did that even though she felt the parent was wrong in his assessment of what was happening in class. Her reflections about these conflicts centered on her questions of what values are appropriate to teach in class and her knowledge that she wasn't "always right."

Again, these two dilemmas illustrate the multiple relationships involved in a classroom; these relationships are not only with students but also with parents, guardians, and others involved in schools. These dilemmas also reveal the importance of talking through the problems. This talking through requires time and highlights the issue of lack of time that Mary, Lesley, and May spoke of previously. The two conflicts described also center on a question of who should have a say in curriculum. In both the dilemmas about teaching state-mandated requirements and the dilemmas where parents wanted a teacher not to teach something, the question of balancing the values of self with those of another, either a parent or a disembodied state, presents a moral dilemma.

How Much Honesty Is Enough?

Another conflict centered on how honest a teacher should be in her conversations with students. When they asked her personal questions, what should she tell them? How much of her life was open for their consideration? What kind of honesty is demanded of a teacher in her relationships with kids? As we talked, one teacher articulated more about these considerations and connections with her students. She said it was a moral question if she couldn't make a connection with her students, for it "might be a waste of a kid's time" if a connection was not made. So her conflict is how to make the connection and, once it is made, what aspects of her experience are open for discussion? She is not a peer and she knows that, but when a student asks an honest question about a moral issue, how should she respond? Is she missing a chance to connect if she doesn't respond in a completely open way? She also worried about when she has the right to change a student's behavior. These are conflicts of values; she felt that if a child was required to come to school and was not able to make a connection with the teacher in his or her class, this lack of connection presented a moral conflict—an absence of a teacher–student relationship.

Yet another teacher, like the two just described, also articulated a conflict that centered on "teaching other people's children," to use Lisa Delpit's

(1995) words. She, too, worried about when to intervene with a student, especially one whose behavior seemed inappropriate to her, and how to leave personal feelings out and treat kids fairly. She wasn't talking about preventing a child from doing something to harm another or something that definitely would be against the rules, but about when was it appropriate to exercise her own values in the classroom.

These three teachers described above articulated dilemmas that recognize differences in their worldview and those held by the children they teach and the parents of these students. This dilemma is one that must be solved over and over. Each time a new student enters a classroom, each time a new school year begins, these questions reappear, so it remains an ongoing dilemma in these teachers' minds.

TALKING ABOUT TEACHING IN AND OUT OF SCHOOLS

We can use the above dilemmas to sketch out a moral landscape using moral terms such as *fairness*, *honesty*, and *rights*. While only one teacher actually used the word *connection* in responding to this question, it is crucial to see these moral ideas embedded in dilemmas of relationship. It is important to recall Piaget's (1932/1965) words, "apart from our relations to other people, there can be no moral necessity" (p. 196). The relationships named in these conflicts are students and parents, and one would expect that. These teachers also spoke of conflicts with colleagues, and one also would expect that. The relationships that might surprise some are those to less intimate others. I would suggest that responsibility to people who describe what should be taught in schools (for example, legislators or state boards of regents) also presents a dilemma. You might think that is really stretching the idea of relationship, but imagine if the person voting on educational law thought he or she was in relationship to a teacher. Remember the way the teacher with the parent dilemmas solved them—she talked. The idea that educators' views and educational research are rarely considered when politicians make educational rules is not a new one. However, I would like to suggest that it is crucial for educational reform that we imagine that these people with disparate stakes in schools are in relationship with the schools. We must begin to speak together about both the academic and the social missions of schooling. It is important to articulate that education for social justice is as important as education for standards. What often is called the hidden curriculum needs to be illuminated, and it can be illuminated by directing our attention to the relationships that are found in classrooms and schools.

These questions provided a starting point for these teachers to talk about themselves and the moral world in their classrooms. While Emily and I were talking, she remarked that she lacked time for reflection and that it was very interesting to have someone really talk to her about what she does. We know that support is crucial for teachers in their professional life (Johnson et al., 2001). We also know that reflection is crucial if teachers are going to continue to develop as good teachers. Yet teachers often are not given the time to reflect with someone else about their work (Hargreaves, 1992).

This has been found over and over by teacher researchers, and it should give pause to those who administer educational institutions. If principals and others would learn to ask questions of teachers, the teachers would have the opportunity to think through what they know and do, and formulate better ways to work with their students. It also might be that asking teachers to think about their work in moral and relational terms would provide all of those concerned with the enterprise of learning new ways to construct that enterprise.

STUDENT INTERACTION

As I mentioned earlier, it was students' interactions with one another that I came to be most interested in and I wanted to know how other teachers thought about this. I asked some teachers to describe their ideal for classroom interactions, and most to talk about the kind of relationships they want their students to develop with one another. The following discussion combines those two questions. The teachers' answers and reflections continue to map the variety of relationships that occur in a classroom and the kinds of relationships they hope to facilitate.

Mary wanted the interaction to give her time "to figure out what they are really asking, or what they really need, as opposed to, you've got 5 seconds of my time and I'm taking a stab at it [understanding what you are asking]." She wanted to be able to have "a real conversation with her students." In other words, she wanted her interactions with students to be meaningful and to help her understand them. She talked about how class size affects her ability to do that. A smaller class presents more possibilities to work individually with each child. Her concerns as she answered this question were with the kind of interaction that gives her the best environment for academic work. Recall the point made earlier about how each of these teachers has high academic standards for her students. Other teachers also focused on academic concerns as they thought about the ideal classroom interaction.

In our conversation about classroom interaction, Chris described the tension she feels between meeting children's affective and cognitive needs. She said, "That's why I'm here to work with the children, [to be] someone they can relate to, someone they are comfortable with"; with someone like that, "they will learn because they are at ease with that person." I want to "ease some of the fears and some of the stress they bring with them, which is out there in their lives, to ease some of that when they walk in." She later said:

> If I can work in positive ways affectively, then I can encourage the children to learn cognitively. Now does that sound like a lot of garbage? If I can create a feeling of well-being, a feeling of warmth, and honest interaction between the adult in the classroom and the 12-year-olds, and if I can encourage the freedom for a student to feel that he or she [can] express themselves, then I think that it is easier for me to start to have them test themselves intellectually and push them intellectually.

Her idea is that our job as teachers is to create a space in which children feel worthwhile enough to risk being wrong (Johnston & Maurer, 2002; Raider-Roth, 2005). This idea connects to the point made earlier in this chapter, that the relationships in a classroom are the ground on which students learn. Chris knows that if students feel comfortable, they will be able to push themselves intellectually and she, too, will be able to push them. They also will be able to express themselves in what she calls an honest interaction.

Throughout our conversations, each of the teachers thought a great deal about classroom relationships. The topic often came up without my prompting it. Molly worked so that students in her art class would not feel isolated. When May talked about this, she spoke of being influenced by the Greenfield School and the work of Charney (2002), and how she wanted to create a real community in her classroom. I will come back to the idea of community in Chapter 6; however, when May talked about it, she said it "had a real strong meaning for her," and she worked to develop that in her classroom. She believed that "community is at the heart of everything

we do and everything we are." Emily, too, addressed this issue by talking
about what kinds of activities go on in elementary schools. "As elementary teachers, I think if you're savvy at all, and if you read at all, and if you
go to conferences and meetings and seminars at all, these kinds of issues
are being talked about all the time among teachers for elementary kids. I'm
not so sure 10, 15 years ago it was done." I asked her what kinds of issues
she meant, and she answered, "Talking about respect and working together
in groups, and talking about cooperativeness, and talking about everybody
working for the same goal, not necessarily winning or beating somebody."
Even as Emily echoed May's ideas about what should happen in a classroom, both wondered whether these kinds of ideas continue beyond elementary school. Is it only when we work with young students that these
ideas are emphasized?

Lesley said she wants kids "giving to each other, thinking about each
other, not just reacting, reflecting with, reflecting about things." She goes
on to say that she teaches them to do this. They work in teams; they do
cooperative tasks, "they get to talk a lot." She also helps them set goals for
this work. "They really have to help each other to do certain tasks. They
can't do it alone." When I asked her why it is important to talk a lot, she
said, "Because they can't guess what somebody's thinking, and when they
know what someone else is thinking, then they can relate to it for themselves." Then she asked, "Is this too mushy?"

Lesley's question goes to the heart of thinking about relationships in
schools. She asks it not because she believes it is "too mushy," but because
she knows that often it is perceived as too mushy. Recall Chris asking, "Does
this sound like a lot of garbage?" Why have we as teachers learned to dismiss a part of teaching that is so crucial to the life of a classroom? I will
discuss this significant question in more detail later.

In answering this question, Mary said, "The objective is to somehow
get them to coexist." She wanted them to be very tolerant of each other. "I
guess ideally, I'd like them to have some sense of working together to accomplish what they need to, of not being in it for themselves. I want the
kids to find the connections to each other." She also wants students to learn
to be independent workers, and for her these goals do not conflict. She
believes kids are always thinking about what "I want" and they need to
think about others, to share ideas and to work together. Chris tried to create a "sense of family" in her classroom; with that sense of family she wants
the kids to have a sense of understanding and tolerance. She said that is
very important and can be "above some of my academic goals."

Molly said she wants students "to be respectful" and set a "rule that you can't put anyone down." Mary, too, established that rule in her classroom, and May said that she couldn't bear it when the kids put one another down. Mary told a story about how exciting it was for her class and herself when her students were able to critique one another respectfully.

> We did thematic readings and had a conversation afterwards about which things stood out. The kids [were] talking [to one another] about it and then also being able to say it didn't work because your head was behind the book, or whatever. [They were] being able to take that back and forth. That was really interesting because when we finished all that discussion, they asked, "Can we do these again?" It is making those kinds of connections where people feel they are recognizing one another. And it is not what you teach. There is such a rich selection of things out there. . . . It is that feeling that you can learn about something and that you can do it if you want to.

When Emily talked about this, she said it was important to her "to see the good in everybody." She struggled to describe why and how that came to be important for her and said that it wasn't always easy for a teacher to find that in every child, but that was her goal for herself and for her class. I quote from our conversation at length because this excerpt gives us two examples of the importance of conversations like this. First, Emily tells us what is important to her, and her words, like those of all the other teachers with whom I have talked, show us the complexity of teachers' thinking. This excerpt is also an example of the interview as a kind of interruption, a space in which someone can think aloud.

> *Emily:* It's hard sometimes for a teacher to always find just that place in kids; it sometimes is difficult to get the kids to see it in each other, but I think we're doing that more and more with collaborative learning, and with using literature to talk about relationships between the story characters, I think all of those things help. And setting goals. You know, all the things that most people, a lot of people, are doing. I think that those things help.
> *Kay:* How do they help the kids specifically, do you think?
> *Emily:* Because they have had a hand in making some of the decisions and rules. Sometimes I direct with the kinds of questions I might ask or something. It's sort of an overused term I suppose,

but it's the ownership. They have had a hand in determining what's to be done.

Kay: Then how does that translate into learning to know the good in one another?

Emily: I think that that the goals almost always have something to do with respect, and with acceptance. I guess they are made more aware of the fact that they need to be accepting and respectful of others and others' ideas. That hopefully in the end helps them to see that there is some good in everybody. I don't know that; I never really talked about that with kids, the good in everybody.

Kay: Do you think you should?

Emily: I'm beginning, yeah. I probably should. That's what made me say that. I really haven't. I've said things like, in talking about other people's ideas, talking about the fact that everybody has good ideas. They might not be the same as yours, you might not agree, but we have to accept what other people think, that kind of thing. But as far as the worth or the good of another, I guess I probably haven't. We talk a lot, maybe it's something I need to do, because we talk about respect, but I'm not sure I've ever actually referred to the good in another person.

The Interview as Intervention

In this interview, Emily is reflecting on her practice. I have already discussed the importance of reflection in the work of teachers. As I talked with her about her beliefs and ideas, she came to see a place where her implicit beliefs may need explicit articulation in her classroom. This is an important point for two reasons. One is that this is exactly what I am trying to do. I want to make our beliefs about and our words for relationships a prominent and explicit part of our educational conversations. These relationships build the context for learning, or, in Bruner's (1996) words, "the culture of education." It is in these relationships that we either take the risk to learn to speak out, or remain passive. Thus, their importance cannot be overstated.

Second, this interview illustrates how paying attention to what someone is thinking helps him or her think more deeply. Recall the description in Chapter 2 of the girl discussing her dilemma about being confused in class. In that conversation she was able to find a new way to think about her problem. In this conversation, Emily thought about something more she might want to say in her classroom. She spoke about how our conversations were a place for her to reflect on her work and how important and unusual this time was. When I was a graduate student working in the Adolescent Project directed by Carol Gilligan, those of us who were on the research team learned to think of the "interview as intervention." By providing a place where a person could be listened to, we provided a place where people could construct alternative ideas about what they were doing and thinking. I think we were paying what Iris Murdoch (1970) called "just attention" (p. 34). I believe this is an activity that is crucial for constructing our ideas and for the development of teachers'—and indeed what Noddings (1992) would call our best—selves. We need to acknowledge that paying attention to others and what they are saying takes time, and this time is crucial for building the relationships that support thinking, reflecting, and taking intellectual risks. This may be one of the most difficult aspects of building relationships in a classroom—it can't be hurried. Yet if we do not acknowledge the time this takes and the importance of building relationships, we may be undermining one of the critical foundations of real thinking.

Building Relationships as a Moral Act

At some point in each of our conversations, I asked each person to define the moral dimensions in her classroom and I also tried to discover whether the relationships just described were part of the moral dimensions in their thinking about teaching. Each teacher described the relational aspect of the classroom as part of the moral dimensions of her teaching.

May cares a great deal about what her students learn, yet she said, "The social curriculum seems a whole lot more important. I feel linked much less to academics and more to social curriculum (sharing, cooperation)." When she knows her students, she learns about each individual and "what they need isn't always reading and writing." She wants to develop the kind of human qualities that you would like to see humans have in life. Lesley said that she felt "school is to learn to look at the world, as we're all part [of it]. We are together in this thing. Then, on top of that comes the academic stuff. People don't talk about this; they think it just happens, and it doesn't. You have to make a conscious effort." Recall Chris saying that sometimes the social curriculum is more important than parts of the academic curriculum.

Lesley's words address the dual goals of school. We have to learn not only the curriculum, which is about material, but also the curriculum that is about how we learn to live together. Again, notice the theme of not talking. She said, "People don't talk about this; they think it just happens." Teachers everywhere know that this doesn't just happen. They know that they must teach their students about working together in the "group life" (Lawrence-Lightfoot, 1988) that is school. Yet, we often don't talk about it unless we are talking about classroom management, discipline, or, worse, the lack of community in school.

Emily, as we learned previously, wants children to see the good in everybody and "hopefully that is built upon in each year." For her that is an important moral aspect of her teaching. Molly spontaneously describes respect as moral. Learning to respect one another and the environment in which students work, and learning to set limits, is the "right thing to do." Mary struggles with the different ideas she holds about morals and values. Initially she said that she thought the moral dimension of a classroom was connected with standards and rules for how to behave, but as she continued our conversation, she said the distinction got hazier for her. Here is part of our conversation:

> *Mary:* One of the things I have noticed that has increased over the years is that kids seem to be more self-centered, and in it for themselves. To me that is not what this whole thing is about. And I'm not saying that it is always doing for each other, but when it happens in your room and you know it is happening, it comes together. It is one of those things that feels like the way it ought to be going. I suppose that is my value, but I think the kids feel good about it when that happens, too.
>
> *Kay:* Is that moral?
>
> *Mary:* I suppose that it is moral if that is the way you view that people ought to exist with each other. If morality is looking at that, then I suppose that it is. Instead of a classroom where each kid comes and is in his corner doing what he needs to do, I want the kids to find the connections with each other.

She went on to explain how she does things outside of class so that kids who aren't as good academically will have opportunities to be recognized— "they get a chance to perform in a different way."

Chris considers her responsibility to the children one of the moral dimensions in her teaching: "We are directly responsible for whether that child is going to have the background to succeed when he or she leaves

school." She also wants children to learn to be tolerant of one another. She
said if "we look at the adult world," one of the problems we have is that
"adults can't get along with other adults." That is a moral problem in her
eyes. May, like Chris and Lesley, gets really angry when kids put one another down. So do Mary and Molly; they all seem to want to establish rules
for this. Gratuitous put-downs are something that shouldn't happen in a
learning/working community. Yet, we must learn to work with people we
don't like and to disagree with one another. I wonder whether these kinds
of conflict can be arbitrated by rules. The question of how to voice a conflict is one to which I return in Chapter 6.

RECURRING RESPONSIBILITIES

Finally, I asked all the teachers to talk about the ideas they continually
revisit in their teaching, "What are the things you keep coming back to—
the recurring themes in your teaching?" Each of these teachers discussed
their responsibility to her students. Each had a different view of that responsibility, but, again, reading their words helps us think about the
sometimes overwhelming responsibility embedded in the relational act
of teaching.

Lesley found herself returning to the "overwhelming responsibility to
do the right thing by them . . . choosing the right thing to teach." By this
she meant "the affective stuff" that an individual or a class needs as well
as the academic curriculum. May said that she worried about "addressing
the needs of the very bright kids." In contrast to Chris, who also worries
about this, May doesn't want them to grow up "expecting stuff to fall into
their hands." In saying this it seems she is concerned not only about their
academic needs, but also about their sense of living in the world. She doesn't
want them to think they are somehow entitled because they are bright. She
wants to treat every child fairly and knows that "fairness and equality are
not the same thing." Emily wondered how to "best teach them. I want them
to learn." Molly worries that kids don't process information as well as they
once did. "They seem more easily pleased and satisfied with minimum
effort in terms of their work. It makes it harder to teach." For Chris the
recurring worry is, how do I get them interested? How do I sustain their
enthusiasm?

As you can see, each of these teachers reflects continually on the work
she does in the classroom. They talk about the tensions they deal with re-

garding their own values and those that they teach students. They wonder about the best way to teach the curriculum and how to teach what
sometimes is called the hidden curriculum or the curriculum that deals with
relational work in a classroom. They think hard about doing the right thing
for their students and they worry about meeting all of the students' needs.
Reading their dilemmas and listening to them describe the moral aspects
of their classroom make clear the relational connections that permeate their
thinking. With this context established for thinking about relationships, we
turn to the words these teachers use to describe the relationships they build.

FOUR

"If I Don't Know My Students, How Can I Teach Them?"

R UTH ELLEN JOSSELSON (1992) explored the meaning of relationship by asking women to describe their relationships in what she called "intensive interviews" (p. xiii). She detailed the meaning of relationship by identifying the dimensions of relationship that women described to her. She identified relational ideas of "yearning, holding, attachment, and mutuality" (p. ix). By describing the meaning of the words these women used to define their relationships, Josselson unpacked the meanings of each word; she made it impossible to collapse the variety of meanings into one simple idea. I use her work as an example of the way the meaning of relationship should be explicated in our work in schools.

We need to be as explicit about the language that describes the dimensions of classroom relationships as Josselson was in her description of the meaning of relationships for the women with whom she worked. Without a map of the dimensions of relationship in classrooms, we obscure the complex dynamics of those relationships. If we obscure those dynamics, relationships might appear to be easily dismissed as only about feelings, and if we think of relationships as only touchy-feely, we undermine their importance. In the previous chapter as Chris was discussing how she wanted the classroom to be comfortable, she looked at me and said, "Does this sound like garbage?" Lesley said that while she knows the importance of her relational activity in her classroom, she won't discuss it with many people because that relational activity becomes "dismissible." Since classroom relationships are the ground on which students' cognitive and ethical activity stands, we cannot dismiss the idea of relationships or their complexity. We need a language that describes the kind of classroom relationships that help us become our best selves morally. This is a necessity in a world that moves so quickly, and in a school world that has become focused on sorting teachers and students on the basis of test scores.

Like Josselson, I have combined the ideas expressed in theory with the reality of relationship expressed in people's interviews. Like her, I believe the word *relationship* has little specific meaning, as I believe the word *community* has little real meaning in the context of schooling. That is not to say individual teachers and theorists don't have a specific meaning for either of those words. I believe they do, but when I think of how the words are used in public conversation, I can't find a meaning.

Josselson points out, and I agree, that relationship has a meaning that is often sexual and usually refers to an intimate relationship. So what are the dimensions of relationships that are not intimate? What words do these teachers use to talk about the interactions in their classroom? What does relationship mean in a situation in which the "relationships" are temporary? Can we have a relationship with someone with whom we will be in contact for less than a year? Can we form a community with people with whom we will be in contact for only a few months? Does that push too far the limits of the ideas those words evoke? The answer to the previous question is, no, but then we have to understand the dimensions of relationships that are only temporary. Do these relationships have the same dimensions as relationships with intimates and others we have grown to know over time?

THE OBJECT IS GETTING THEM TO COEXIST

As these teachers talked about the kinds of relationships they wanted their students to develop with one another, it was apparent that they thought hard about facilitating students' interactions.

Mary, quoted earlier, said, "The objective is to somehow get them to coexist." She wanted them to be very tolerant of each other. "I guess ideally, I'd like them to have some sense of working together to accomplish what they need to, of not being in it for themselves. I want the kids to find the connections to each other."

Each of these teachers wants a classroom in which students learn to work with one another. They work toward that end, but the teaching strategies of cooperative learning and group work do not describe the interpersonal work and the thinking that make these strategies possible. To understand that, one must understand that putting a group of students together, either in a small group or even in a classroom, requires much more than giving them a meaningful task. It requires teaching them what kind of interpersonal work goes into cooperative academic work.

An explicit description of this interpersonal work is missing from our descriptions of classrooms. To begin to explain this, each of the teachers used a variety of words that describe the kinds of relationships they both find and seek to develop in their classrooms. Therefore, each teacher has a variety of theories about what is necessary in order for students to learn from and with one another. Each theory is expressed in the words they chose to describe classroom relationships. Their words make clear that the idea of relationship is not simply one aspect of school; it is, in reality, many.

RELATIONSHIPS AS THE CONTEXT
FOR MORAL ACTION: THE WORDS WE USE

If we take seriously the idea that schooling is relational and that relationships are the context for cognitive and moral behavior, then we begin to see the importance of thinking about building relationships as moral activity. Defining morality in this way reveals the essential moral dimension of classrooms. We must learn not only the information that is part of the academic curriculum, but also to practice being together in respectful ways. When we debate what some might call moral issues—for example, should we or should we not distribute condoms in school—and call that morality, we miss the essential goal of living a moral life. That goal is to live with others. This is not a morality of values that we simply transmit to students; it is a morality of interaction. Relational morality encompasses the ideas of both justice and care, as described in Chapter 2. Relational morality urges us to reflect on a situation and to act in a way that maintains connections with people and that treats everyone with fairness. If we begin to understand the dimensions of relationships in a classroom, we will begin to understand and practice ways of living together that are both just and caring.

The words that title the following sections were used by the teachers with whom I spoke. The words were often used in the discussions about moral dilemmas in the classroom described in the previous chapter, so in some cases the words take us back to a context with which we are already familiar. However, as you will see, though the dilemmas may be familiar, the meaning of each of these words may not be. Each of the teachers used many of the same words, but often differently. The meanings they give to words exemplify new ways to understand the interactions that occur in classrooms. If ten students were asked to name a word that described how they would like their teachers to treat them, most of them would say that they wanted teachers to be "fair." It is a word that begins the discussion of the dimensions of classroom relationships.

"Fair"

Three of the teachers used the word *fair* in our conversations. I would like to first illustrate how they used that word and then discuss the variety of theories the word *fair* represents. As previously discussed, one of the moral conflicts described by a teacher centered on an issue of fairness. It was a moral problem to not challenge the very bright kids in the class. "I don't think that is fair to them." The unfairness involved in this is teaching subject material that does not challenge the top kids, but "turns them into teachers" for the kids who aren't as bright.

This worry occurs because the teacher sees a contradiction in heterogeneous grouping; it is good for what we have referred to as the social curriculum, but not as good for the academic. Another teacher speaks about fairness as it relates to grouping, and worries that all students "aren't getting a fair shake." Some of that worry comes because she fears that the very bright children "are learning that they don't have to work very hard at anything."

Both of these uses of the word *fairness* seem to bring up issues of equity and equality. In fact, in discussing what she believes is fair in relation to the issues she raises, the second teacher provided her own definition when she said, "Fairness and equity are not the same thing." Both teachers think hard about what it means to treat everyone with fairness within an academic framework. Regardless of which view you find more in line with your own view of heterogeneous grouping, it is obvious that the meaning of fairness as it is used in these conversations is one that most of us would think of immediately.

I am struck by the idea of fairness in one teacher's thinking. After defining the difference between equity and sameness, she says that she wants to give every kid the best, she wants to treat everyone fairly in that she gives each child what that child needs. She works hard at that and sometimes feels overwhelmed by the reality of that task. My sense is that also is why the first teacher quoted above finds that fairness is an issue. Here is one of the contradictions that is a daily fact in teachers' lives: To challenge all kids to work at their highest level, a teacher must work very hard. Sometimes the reality of the multiple levels of student ability in one class makes it seem impossible to do. Embedded in this view of fairness in relationship is a reality that treating everyone the same can't be done. One teacher wondered how to do this when some of the children are more privileged than others. Because of economic privilege, some of the children she teaches have many more enriching experiences outside of the classroom. Do these children deserve more attention in class?

When she was describing herself as a teacher, Emily said, "One of the most important things [about her teaching] is being fair." At first I thought that meant what the two teachers quoted above meant—treating everyone fairly—and certainly there was an element of that in her idea. She went on, however, to elaborate that being fair meant to "give everybody a chance, to give everybody a chance to tell me what they think." She believes that being heard allows each child "to feel worthwhile, no matter who they are." This goal presented problems for her in her classroom because she didn't always know when to stop discussions. When should she assume everyone has had their say, and when should she wait a few seconds longer? Again, this question illuminates the myriad decisions that teachers make when they are teaching and it is certainly a question of equity. But Emily puts a new twist on it: She wants to connect fairness with the idea of voice—it is fair to make sure she lets each child talk, for that "allows kids to have an equal chance in the classroom."

The dimensions of fairness found in these excerpts are (1) treating people equally or treating a variety of people with equity in a classroom, and (2) giving everyone the chance to talk. The first focuses on how the teacher instructs students, and the second focuses on how the teacher provides for the students' voice. These are not mutually exclusive, but they do enlarge the domain of the theory of fairness, and the latter definition brings the idea of relationships into focus. This is important because the idea of fairness often is equated with the idea of justice and may not be connected explicitly to relationship.

One other dimension in Emily's discussion of what it means for her to be fair is that she wonders about being unfair to a child if she has become stern. When she does become stern in her classroom, she sees the children pull together. Piaget (1932/1965) wrote about this phenomenon, which he called solidarity among children. He said that when the adult is clearly the authority, the children pull together and act "in solidarity" against the adult. For example, they might not tell the adult who is responsible for some infraction of the rules. Obviously, there are times in a responsible adult's interaction with children that call for firmness. Emily, however, notices what that does to her classroom and it is a point worth pondering.

I go back to my experience with my students. The students in the cheating incident structured that dilemma so that their options were to be silent or to tell me, the authority. Have our students learned that solidarity, that pulling together, because they haven't learned to see the teacher in connection to the class? In other words, most students understand that they can have a relationship with a teacher and that the teacher can have relationships with others in the class. I wonder whether students have learned, however, that the teacher is not only an authority, but also a member of the temporary relationship that is the classroom. If they have not learned that, it is easier to separate the authority from the classroom community and not to think complexly about the interactions involved in that community. If students don't see everyone, including the teacher, as a member of the community, it is simple to develop an us-versus-them mentality —students versus teacher.

I have begun elaborating on words that fit with the idea of justice, as described in the coding scheme outlined in Chapter 2, in the sense of how justice might be used to regulate relationships and not as an abstract idea used to adjudicate problems. Another word that seems to connect with justice is *right*. Often we think of right as having to do with what a person is owed or entitled to, such as the right to privacy. In the following discussions, the idea of right lines up more with another commonsense notion, that there is a right thing to do, even though it is not always exactly clear who defines that right thing. The next section looks at the teachers' words that explain the multiple layers of right behavior in a relationship.

"Right"

In the United States today, there are many contradictory voices arguing that they know what is right for everyone. What does right mean when used in the context of the relational world of a classroom? May said she knows she isn't always right. "I don't have all the answers," yet she talks about having to do the right thing when she thinks about the dilemmas she faces in her work. She says, "I have to do the right thing here," but for her the right thing is not a single action, but the activity of dialogue. "The right thing is to talk about this." Her idea is that the right thing to do is to communicate; even when she feels that she doesn't agree with the other person, she still feels it is necessary to talk about the situation. This idea of dialogue is one that Noddings (1992) discusses in terms of care, and for May it is essential in terms of solving the dilemmas embedded in her practice.

Chris says she has a sense of doing what is right with kids. She describes this sense as creative, not really following rules. While we often judge what is right by some standard outside of ourselves, Chris argues that there is "a kind of feel, like a painter might have, about what is right to do."

Lesley uses the word in a similar way when she talks about "doing what is right by them." She wants to do "right" by her students and she thinks about the many competing issues against which she must decide what is right. Recall one teacher's dilemma of not having enough time to do all that is required and all that she wants to accomplish. She says she only has them for a little bit of time and wants to do the right things in this short amount of time. Lesley said something that is quite profound in the context of discussing what is right for her students. She said that she must "choose the right things to teach," and contrasted this with "teaching the things right." She meant that she wanted to and often did choose what previously has been referred to as the social curriculum as the "right thing" to teach a particular group of students. This is similar to May's saying that the social curriculum can be more important for some children than the academic one.

When Mary considers questions of right and wrong, she asks what right she has as a teacher to push her own ethical agenda.

> But then you look at basic things that you expect of the kids in terms of relating to each other and things like that. I think about that, what things do you have a right to impose on kids?

Then she brings up the point of not connecting with a kid and wondering, "At what point do you have the right to waste the kids' time every day? And how do you have the right to set out to change a kid's behavior?"

For Emily, doing the right thing is to make sure her feelings don't get in the way of treating everyone fairly. She has a goal for her students and herself and that "goal is to see good in everybody. I mean, I can rant and rave about certain politicians and whatever, but when it comes right down to it, there is some good in everybody. So, that's what I want for those kids—for each of them to see that in the other kid." She elaborates about how hard it can be for a teacher to always find that place in kids: "It sometimes is difficult to get the kids to see it in each other." So, for Emily, doing the right thing, being right in class, is to get the children to understand that there is good in everyone; she explicitly links this to a moral standard.

This is reminiscent of a discussion Mary and I had about children learning to respect and to see the worthiness of others' ideas. She works on this happening, especially in discussions about the values students find in the literature they read. As Emily and I talk about the right thing being the ability to see the good in everybody, she reflects that this is her goal, but she can't remember sharing it explicitly with her students. Emily said, "I never really talk about that with kids, the good in everybody." This is a point to which I will return.

For Molly, it is very hard to have the time to talk about issues of what is right and wrong outside the context of behavior in her classroom. She wants the children to understand that there is a limit to the resources they have, and that "it is wrong to misuse" supplies and equipment. She also sets standards of behavior in her room, but as an art teacher who has many students in a week, she worries she doesn't know the kids very well and she might misinterpret them.

> I'll say you can't make weapons, you can't make guns, you can't make knives, because they hurt people and there's enough violence and enough horrible things happening in the real world that we don't need [it to] happen in the art room, too. To me that is making a moral stand. I have no problems setting that kind of limit, but I don't know why it's hard for me to actually confront a kid about doing something that I feel really goes over the line of what I think is okay. It is different to think of the rules of the room and to confront a particular kid. The rules of the room are nonspecific to a child.

This is an interesting dilemma for a teacher who might teach 500 or more students in a year. As we saw, she doesn't want students to feel isolated and she works to know each child, but knowing each child is very difficult given the student load she has. For Molly, relationship-building with students is "the right thing to do," but she isn't sure she is convinced that it is a moral consideration. She also wants them to understand the right way to behave in a classroom that is used by hundreds of students each week.

Again in these uses of the word *right*, we see a variety of meanings. Sometimes right is linked to standards of "right behavior" and sometimes it is linked to action, and these meanings might be predicted. It is significant that May and Emily lead us explicitly to the ideas of relationship in their use of the word *right*. For May, doing the right thing is to communicate, and for Emily, it is to learn to see the good in everybody. All the teachers implicitly think of the word in the context of relationship because behaving in the right way can be judged only in relation to those with whom you are behaving.

"Respect"

Another word several teachers used to describe the kinds of relationships that they wanted their students to develop was *respect*—they wanted their students to be respectful of one another. When we think of the way that respect is used in descriptions of relationships we develop, most of us might think of mutual respect. It is the commonsense notion of respect that is examined by Piaget, who says that as we develop and learn to cooperate, we learn mutual respect for our peers. What do these teachers really mean when they use this word?

May began her interview by describing herself as a teacher who is very interested in developing the "social curriculum" in her classroom. When I asked her what that social curriculum entailed, she replied, "Umm, sharing, cooperation, respect for one another, kind of human qualities that you would like to see humans have in life. And those are the things that I like to foster in the classroom." I asked her how she fostered those qualities.

> I do a lot of talking about it. One of the things that I decided lately is not to assume anything. And then I teach those things directly. I teach listening skills. When somebody is talking, you do just what you're doing—you look into their eyes, you nod your head to show that [you are listening]. These are behaviors that are positive behaviors. I think that's it: teaching it directly, not to assume that they know these things. I see kids get yelled at a lot for not doing things, and they haven't been taught.

In this excerpt you hear May beginning to talk about the community she tries to develop in her classroom; for her, respect is linked to listening and behavior. She thinks it is important to tell her students what she expects of them. This is reminiscent of the way Vygotsky discusses learning. The external becomes internalized, and May is trying to provide external examples of behavior that is fundamentally moral, at least in the Western culture in which she teaches.

For Emily, "respect is equated with acceptance." She was described above as thinking aloud that she didn't believe she ever talked with the kids about "finding the good in everybody." In her reflections about respect, she said she did explicitly talk to the children about this. She described the children making the rules for the room.

> I think the goals almost always have something to do with respect, and with acceptance. I guess they are made more aware of the fact that they need to be accepting of others and others' ideas and be respectful of them. . . . I tell them everybody has good ideas. They might not be the same as yours, you might not agree, but we have to accept what other people think. That kind of thing.

This meaning of respect refers to a way of receiving another person's ideas. This is similar to but not exactly like the behavior that May was trying to develop in her students. Emily realizes that all ideas aren't necessarily good ones, but she says that her students learn from hearing both good and bad ideas and "receiving those ideas." Learning must begin with entertaining the possibility that a new idea, an idea that is different from the ideas one has, might be a good one, so Emily's objective regarding respect for new ideas seems the place to start learning and evaluating that learning. Her desire to have her students "accept what other people think" does not mean that ultimately they must believe others' ideas, but that they must be open to the notion that there is a way to see and understand both words and experiences that is different from the way they see and understand.

In answering the questions about the kinds of relationships she wants her students to have, the first word Molly used was "respectful." She went on at some length to describe what she means by respect.

> I want all kids to feel that they can come in and do it [art]. You see, so much of what kids do is right out there in art. . . . I have kids [with] a wide range of ability. One kid may have poor eye-hand control or doesn't really have much talent or skill . . . and he or she could be sitting next to the next Picasso. I don't want that kid who has less ability to feel bad, to feel that their work is any less valuable or any less valued. So that's something that I've tried to help kids with. You can't put anyone else down. I don't use those words, but I give all kids opportunities—no matter who they are—to talk about their work. When we get into a group situation [and] we're talking about work, everyone has the right to be respected . . . not to be put down in any way. You know, kids will bring that up at the beginning of the year when we talk

about what kind of rules we need in the art room. Someone will say
that "you can't say anything bad about other people's work," and I'll
say, "That's right, you can't. If you want to talk about someone else's
work you can. You can talk about all kinds of things. You can talk
about the color, you can talk about what they made, you can talk
about how they made things and people can explain things to you. But
to turn and say someone else's work is not good is not okay." And I
think that's part of being respectful to each other. This is part of their
morals. I think people are just really negative to each other. I feel really
strongly about that. As I say to kids, you don't have to like everything,
you don't have to like things; I'm asking you to think about what you
don't like. It's just thinking about what someone else might feel. I think
that's really important, I really do. And I just don't think kids get
enough of it—thinking about what someone else wants or needs.

This teaching about how someone might respond to an evaluation
of their work is like Emily's notion of respecting ideas, but in this interview Molly adds an additional dimension, which she calls moral. This
dimension adds thinking about the consequences of one's interactions to
May's notion of listening. Molly's ideas about respect explicitly add the
notion of perspective-taking, which all of the preceding excerpts deal with
implicitly.

As noted earlier, Molly also is trying to get the kids to understand what
it means to respect materials. She tries to teach the children in her art room
to treat the materials respectfully because "there is limit to what we have."
So she introduces an inanimate object of respect—the material with which
the children work. This is similar to Noddings's (1992) idea of learning to
care about the classroom and the environment.

The words discussed so far usually are thought of in relation to the
moral orientation of justice. As the variety of meanings of these words
become clearer and more complex, we get a better understanding of how
these "justice words" function in relationships that are built in the classroom. Sometimes these words are connected explicitly to the classroom
relationship and sometimes it is an implicit connection, yet the connection
is there. Now we turn to other words that teachers used in these interviews;
these words are more obviously words used in the care orientation, but
again the complexity of the meanings of these words negates a simple cor-
relation of the meaning of a word with only one orientation.

"Community"

It might seem as if community would be the key word for this book. We use this word a lot as a culture. Think about the discussions over loss of community since the book *Habits of the Heart* (Bellah et al., 1985) was published. I have been trying to notice when the word *community* is used in the media to describe education, and it seems for the most part to be used as a negative descriptor; there is usually a lamenting about the lack of community when the media report incidents at school, especially tragedies like school shootings. In literature about schooling, however, we find this word used extensively. The following excerpts express both negative and positive ideas about community.

Recall May's saying she was influenced by Ruth Charney's work. Charney (2002) has written extensively about ways to develop caring communities, but spends less time exploring what the word *community* means. May says that a community of care is "at the heart of not only what we do, but everything we are." She elaborates on the importance of community in her classroom.

> Their [Charney and the Greenfield School] main focus is the social curriculum and how it, in turn, affects society. And what they deal with is respect for one another and there's a lot of responsibility put on the kids right away for that respect. They're taught how to do it, and when they're engaged in conversation, they do a lot of imagery. You know, "Imagine how you would feel, what would it be like if you were?"

There is no doubt that this is the center of the social curriculum in May's room. May believes that the community she is talking about really exists in most primary-grade classrooms and that it gets lost as kids get older. It is interesting to think about this last statement. Emily, perhaps, says something similar. When I told her what my students said about when they asked a question in class, Emily thought that younger kids wouldn't think about questions as an act of competence as my students did. This presents a question about the structure of schooling. Is it only little children who are willing to take risks in class?

Roberta Simmons (1987) wrote that the structure of schools works against developing relationships in adolescence. And the current research on schools shows that smaller schools are the best environment for adolescent development (Meier, 2002). Even as we develop schools within schools, are we working against ourselves if we are not explicit with our students about the relationships needed for these schools to function successfully?

This question, then, of the importance of community is critical in thinking about education. Yet, May is the only teacher who uses that word in a positive way. Molly said that *community* seems to be a favorite "buzzword of administrators," and she worried it didn't have any meaning; however, she wanted that feeling in her classroom, a feeling May described as nice and warm: "I want kids to feel comfortable, I want them to feel that it's their place [room] when they're there and I guess that's a part of caring. When the kids come in, they're mine, they're my kids—they're my responsibility for that 40-minute period." That has real meaning for her.

Lesley, too, believes that developing that sense of comfort, of warmth "is a big deal, but to talk about it seems too mushy." At one point in our conversation, Chris was talking about a sense of being together with her students and worried that she sounded "too much like a braggart," when she talked about this. This sense of unease about this "feeling" is worth thinking about as we consider what other things teachers had to say about developing a sense of being a cohesive group in a classroom.

Mary discussed getting "kids to coexist." Sometimes that means that one or more children "need to change their outlook, or their behavior or something, or just expand their acceptance." This needs to be done when their behavior affects the other kids. This coexistence relates to the earlier discussion prompted by one teacher's asking, "What right do I have to change someone else's behavior?" As she thought about the way children behave with one another, the bottom line for Mary was that she wanted her students to "be very tolerant of each other. I guess ideally I'd like them to have some sense of working together to accomplish what they need to, of not being in it for themselves."

The sense of "not being in it for themselves only" is the essence of the feeling that May called community and that all of the teachers thought was very important in their classrooms. These teachers want their students to understand that education is not only about what they learn, but also about how they learn to think about the others involved in their classroom. This means learning about living and working together and about the fact that they are responsible for themselves and for their student colleagues.

"Sense of Family"

Chris is the only teacher who actually used this phrase to describe what she hopes her classroom has.

> I guess it comes down to what I hope to achieve in the classroom with the group of children that I have for the year. . . . [One] of the goals I have with my group is to develop a sense of family in here—we are here together, we work together. [Another is] a sense of understanding and tolerance, [these] are above some of my academic goals.

This seems to be only in Chris's vocabulary; she means creating a sense of warmth, a sense of working together that is like the "feeling of community" May described or the comfortable feeling Molly talked about. Chris said if she creates this "sense of family," the students "can test themselves intellectually and I can push them intellectually." This "sense of family" creates a safe space for the intellectual challenges in a classroom.

While other teachers don't talk about creating a sense of family, they use family terms to describe their teaching. May said that she feels like a mommy or a grandmother, and Mary described herself as feeling like a mother in her classroom. Lesley said she wants her class to be cozy, like a home. This is similar to Martin's (1992) idea of the schoolhome. However, another way to think about the use of family terms and ideas of home to describe teaching may connect with what I said earlier. The terms in our vocabulary that we use to describe relationships are terms most often connected with relationships that are intimate. Perhaps if we think of schooling as relational, we can enlarge the domain of terms used to describe how important these relationships are. If we acknowledge public relationships, we may learn to describe them in ways other than those used to describe more intimate relationships.

"Caring"

This is the word most often used to describe the connections that we have with other people. Both Gilligan and Noddings use this word to describe a way of being that initially was associated with women. I have described Gilligan's work in Chapter 2. Noddings (1984, 1992, 2002) has written much about this ethic and has been very influential in bringing this idea into the domain of schooling. It is instructive, however, to see the meaning of this term as it is used by the teachers in this study.

Lesley describes herself as a caring teacher and that means she tries to "adapt myself to what my students need." She learns about that "by watching them, by talking to their parents, and listening to them a lot, by asking them a lot of questions." In fact, caring for another demands paying attention, and all good teaching requires this kind of care. Lesley extends the watching and listening beyond academic concerns to trying to find out how students are doing emotionally in her class. It is in this discussion that she talks about the contradiction referred to earlier. She says that teachers "have to believe that they [their students] might never get another teacher who cares about them so much, yet you have the faith they will [find another teacher who cares for them as much]."

In addition to caring for her students, Lesley also talks about wanting them to learn to care for one another. She refers to this as the "my brother's keeper thing." She talked about this in a context already quoted, but it is worth listening to again. She worries about "teaching the right things." "It is an enormous responsibility choosing the right things to focus on." I asked her, "What would those be?"

> For me, a lot of affective stuff. Kids learning how to question things and feeling good about that, but also a lot of interacting with the world. I have a strong sense that I really want them to be involved in community service. . . . Because it's that whole thing of my brother's keeper, and I feel as a teacher that's part of who I am, and I feel that they need to be that for everybody.

She explicitly teaches the word empathy and returns to that idea many times in many ways during the year. She helps the children set little goals and reach them.

> I have to teach them how to do that. . . . You know I really believe that I am giving them a basis for their whole life. I don't think that a lot of people talk about it, or really focus on [making] it a goal for themselves with their kids. I don't think people think about it. They think it just happens. I don't think it just happens; you have to make a conscious effort. I mean, it has to be something that you think about and work with kids on. I think that they have to be thinking about it.

Notice the juxtaposition of two ideas in Lesley's words. One idea is learning how to question things and feeling good about that, and the second is interacting with the world. When she connects the ideas of intellectual questioning and caring for others, we hear echoes of Chris saying that if she can create a "sense of family," she can challenge her students more. In both cases, we do not have a dichotomy of creating either a feel-good classroom or a challenging one, but the reality that intellectual challenges are more likely to be taken seriously if we trust those who are challenging us. Thus the importance of creating a classroom in which students can learn to be in relationship with one another has both emotional and intellectual impact. Also notice Lesley's emphasis on being explicit about this goal with her students. She works on it in different ways throughout the year, helping them define goals that will help them interact in "empathetic" ways with other children.

Lesley also talks of caring in another way. When she talked about "learning from people who care to struggle," she was discussing what has been recognized as the isolation many teachers feel. She tries to learn from other teachers, but she finds that she can't learn from folks who aren't really working hard at the issues, both academic and social, with which she is concerned. In describing who those people are, she says they must care enough about the work to struggle. She is describing the kind of "stick-to-it-ness" that one must have in the face of difficulty.

For me, her idea of caring enough to struggle is a feeling that we don't often nurture in schools. I worry we want to "know what the answer is" whether we are students or teachers, and the time it takes to care enough to struggle isn't valued. This isn't the traditional notion of caring in relationship, but it is a significant aspect of caring. If one is working to pay attention to a particular person or issue, then one must care enough to struggle with the complexities that a human being or a learning situation inevitably will hold.

Emily said she constantly thinks about and plans for "them wanting to learn and to love learning." In this she echoes Chris. She also thinks constantly about teaching them "to care about each other, be supportive of each other, feel some responsibility for each other in a way." Again, this is a teacher's concern for developing connections among the students in a class, and again, it isn't simply a feel-good idea, but an idea about responsibility for one another.

Molly said:

> I read once that what parents want is for their kids to be liked and to
> be cared for, and to be treated well, with some special feeling. I think

that's true. I think kids want to be special, so they want to make sure that they make a difference, perhaps. So for me, knowing kids and making some kind of connection with kids when I teach them, is a message to them that I care about them.

She also used the term *caring* to describe the relationship that the children in regular education develop with the special education kids in her art class: "Kids are very thoughtful." She tries not to let kids "be isolated." She told a story about a special needs child who was being fully included in a classroom that was not special needs. She had had some difficulty in past years with this boy and he also had difficulty with other students. She needed some help at the end of the day putting up heavy chairs and she asked the kids if someone could help her.

This boy, John, took it upon himself to be in charge of this job. Everyday, without fail, he has corralled these little kids into the art room. Some days it is just John and another kid. He's got them all timed, so they have records of how fast they do it. One day I said to him, "How do you know how fast you're doing this, you can't possibly know?" And this other kid said, "Oh yeah, he just starts counting. Show her."

She went on to describe how John really developed that year.

So that's been kind of a neat thing. That sense of being able to have a kid change so much, and develop positive relationships within the class, and how that really has impacted his life in a very major way. The kids really have accepted him in a way he wasn't expecting them to.

She continued that this change wasn't simply because of her, but that she was part of it and she was touched by the way the children were "thoughtful" about this little boy who was clearly different from them.

"Connecting"

Mary uses the word *connecting* to talk about relationships in her room. Her ideal classroom has fewer kids than her actual classroom; it is her ideal because she wants "to connect with each kid." In Chapter 3 Mary is quoted as describing a wonderful lesson in which the kids were talking about a book they had been reading. In that lesson the kids were "being able to take the back and forth" that occurs in a real dialogue. It was exciting because the students were connecting and talking about both what they liked and what they didn't like. It is instructive that she feels this is not a constant occurrence in the classroom, but that when it happens she feels wonderful about those times. It is also important to see that the students are not just talking about the good things. This is a back and forth, and the description sounds different from the times when kids aren't allowed to say something critical about one another's work.

Molly instantly described herself as someone who tries to "make some kind of personal connection with kids and that's really hard to do but it's something I care about," because "if I don't know my students, how can I teach them?" This sounds like Lesley and May watching and listening to get to know their students, to make a connection with them. "If I don't know my students, how can I teach them?" This sense of knowing, of connection, is so obvious in each of these teachers' words. They illuminate the importance not only of knowing the students but also of providing a sense of ease in a classroom so that students can be helped to be their best selves, both intellectually and personally. Seeing the spontaneity with which teachers talk about creating these connections, it seems odd that we don't always talk about teaching and learning as relational.

These ideas of caring and connecting link to a sense of trust that can be the context for real learning. One of the teachers discussed a moral dilemma she experienced when a child stole something in her classroom. She had trusted the students and it was painful to learn about the stealing. This connected for me with my own feeling of betrayal when some of my students cheated. Trust is something one thinks of in connection to people one knows, yet Lesley said she had to trust that other teachers would care as much about her students as she did. Trust must extend beyond the classroom to teachers she knows and to others who are not known to her. Thus trust becomes a feeling that is necessary in order to teach. In the words of these teachers, it is necessary for learning as well as the basis for relationships.

"Collaboration"

Collaboration is a word that needs serious consideration in the development of a relational language for schooling. For four of the teachers with whom I spoke, this word evoked ideas about the difficulty they faced in collaborating with colleagues. Two of them spoke directly about how they were more cautious now in what they said or did in relation to their profession. This was both in and out of class. One said that she was more reluctant to share ideas with other teachers because she didn't feel she was reciprocally treated. Not wanting to be unprofessional, none of the teachers would go into details, but all of them talked about the influence of other teachers and administrators. These influences were both good and bad.

It is interesting that even as each of these teachers talked about connecting and caring, of their concern for the students, and how the students learn from one another, no one really talked about the problems of collaboration for the students in their classroom. Each of them took the opportunity to think about herself as a collaborator and the difficulties inherent in that work. Embedded in the word itself is the word *labor*. In my view, the labor involved in collaboration is the labor involved in relationship. Specifically, I think that it is labor to work together and to share ideas. It is such an obvious point that we can't always get what we want when we truly work together. There are disagreements and different views, and there is inevitably compromise. The teachers who spoke of being more cautious, of being silenced, present a response that is often the result of this labor. It is the response that stymied me in my work with my own students because they could not find a way to express their disapproval to their friends. This silencing is what might be avoided by creating a sense of community, or of family, a feeling of warmth, but the difficulty in this needs to be acknowledged or we will be unable to have a real dialogue. I will return to that point in Chapter 6.

There are some words that we might expect everyone to use when thinking about moral dimensions of teaching. When I began this project, I had the idea that words like *responsibility*, *cooperation*, and *democratic* might be used; however, they were used much less often than I had predicted. Three of the teachers wanted their students to develop some responsibility for one another and for the classroom, and they did think hard about what that meant, but it was not the word that most of them used to describe the work in their classrooms. All of them did use that word when they were considering how to make decisions about their teaching. They said in various ways that they wondered what their responsibility was to present certain material and their own views about certain subjects.

Cooperation was used by one teacher to describe the behavior she wanted to see her kids engage in, and by another to describe the kinds of ideas about learning that permeate teacher inservice. The word *democratic* was only used once, by Lesley when she described how she is less democratic than she used to be. By that she means she feels more confident about laying out the rules and work to be done and less likely to negotiate everything that goes on in her class.

The process of sketching out the meanings of the relational words used by the teachers in this study has called the complexity of these relationships to our attention. While each teacher uses the words in similar ways, defining them has uncovered the differences in how these words come to have meanings for these teachers, and once again calls into question assumptions we make about knowing what people think about classroom community. We might have predicted that everyone would use community to describe their classroom, but only one person actually used that word in a positive way. We might not have predicted that the word *democratic* would be used only as a descriptor and in the context of how a teacher had become less democratic, which meant less willing to negotiate about what kinds of work got done in class. In addition, thinking about the self-descriptions of these teachers and the moral conflicts they describe provides a context for these relational words. The next question becomes, What importance do these words and conflicts hold for other teachers? Why bother thinking about this?

FIVE

An Awesome Responsibility

E DUCATING OTHER people's children is an awesome responsibility (Donaldson, 1978). I hope I have convinced you it is fundamentally a moral responsibility. Yet, as Ken Tobin (1991) points out, "The moral dimension of teaching is invisible." It is important to think about this for the reasons outlined in Chapter 1. In my own work I was confronted by a dilemma in my students' behavior; I was surprised by how much power the students had to silence one another in both the academic and the moral arena. Students reported they didn't ask questions for fear of looking dumb, and students told me they didn't know how to talk with one another about how to handle a difficult issue of cheating.

PROBLEMS IN RELATIONSHIPS

On one hand, I wasn't surprised to learn how effective this silencing is, but on the other hand, I was flabbergasted. These are young adults, and my hope as a teacher is to contribute to the development of young people who can be responsible, moral citizens in an increasingly complex world. Yet, I did not know how to break through that silencing.

A central question in this cheating dilemma was the fact that some of the students talked about being friends with some of the students who presented the problem to them. Why can't we talk about these hard things in a classroom? Thinking about that question, I look at my own behavior and explore when I feel okay about speaking up. I look at these teachers' stories and see some of them talking about becoming more cautious and all of them talking about relational dilemmas in their teaching. Sometimes the difficulty of speaking up, of recognizing a conflict, comes in relationships with students, for example, Molly talking about the difficulty of confronting individual students when she feels she doesn't know them well and might misinterpret their behavior. Sometimes these conflicts are with parents, as when one of the teachers described a moral dilemma in which she was misunderstood by a parent. And sometimes the moral dilemma is with a colleague, either teacher or administrator. Although I did not describe them because of ethical considerations regarding the privacy of all involved, every teacher had a version of this dilemma. All of these dilemmas were embedded in relationships, and the solutions often resulted in silencing of one sort or another.

So to return to my question, What difference does it make if we begin to acknowledge the complicated relational dilemmas that permeate schooling? I think we need to confront not only the positive aspects of relationships but also the negative ones. One of the obvious negative aspects of relationships is the possibility that an individual isn't really in a dialogue in the relationship. That can happen when an individual always defers to the other person, or when an individual doesn't recognize that another person might have a different idea about something. Both of these are problems of perspective. The first, as Gilligan (1982) suggests, loses track of the self, for lack of a better term, and the second loses track of the other. Both losses of perspective are problems in relationship.

Do problems in relationship really affect what happens in a classroom? My answer is yes, and we need to think about what we can do to address those problems. Lesley said that teachers need to teach empathy. She doesn't think it just happens; it needs to be practiced. I believe that idea is key to this work. We, as teachers, need to think about teaching, practicing, and modeling the behavior we would like to see our students and even ourselves use in social relationships, both when these relationships feel comfortable and when they are in conflict. This kind of work begins with our thinking about relationships and then has the potential to influence our behavior. Vygotsky believed that what one learns with assistance today, one can do alone tomorrow. This is, of course, his famous zone of proximal development. Jerome Bruner (1996) wrote, "Knowledge helps only when it descends into habits" (p. 152). They both are talking about how we learn, and I am talking about how we learn to think about ourselves in the multiple relationships we experience in schools.

THE ACHIEVING SELF

In our schools we have a goal of developing an achieving self—that is, a self who competes and works hard as an individual—and we have some pretty good models for that kind of self. That is an important model for our children. We also know that not every child can be that kind of self. We know that issues of race, class, gender, and sexual orientation can impede that achievement, but we also know we have that model. That is the model that is lionized and mythologized in our culture. This is the person who gets ahead, sometimes against all odds. This is the person who does well on the tests, who stands out in the class, on the athletic field, and in many other areas of achievement. Of course, the problem with that self is that the achievement can come at the cost of others. We know there can be only one number one in a group. Now, I don't believe anyone would say that there shouldn't be competition or that someone should give up his or her own achievement because it may leave others behind. What I do believe is that achievement must be recognized as having both benefits and costs. It doesn't mean that relationships don't involve competition; it simply means that the results of competition must be recognized as occurring in a relationship. Competition occurs in a social context.

THE SOCIAL SELF

Another self for whom we have a model is the self in relationship. This self usually is constructed in connection to an "other" who is an intimate—a partner, a friend, a lover, a child. What we need is a model for a self in other kinds of relations. Dewey called them social relations, so let's call that a social self. This social self is not a self that we construct at social engagements, although that self is one about which we could talk at length. This social self is the self we find in associations that may be temporary, but are intense encounters. I speak of the self we find in classrooms, in meetings, and, I would say, in a democratic society. In this chapter I will limit my discussion to the student self as it might be constructed in a relationship. I will leave the student–teacher relationship to others for now and concentrate on how teachers must learn to think about developing a student self who is able to participate in rich relationships with other student selves. I have called this the student–student relationship and I believe it is facilitated by a thoughtful teacher.

THE STUDENT–STUDENT RELATIONSHIP

I would like to make clear that I think all teachers think about this. Every teacher who talked with me spoke about the kind of "community" she wanted in her classroom. However, what interests me is the idea that we need to be more explicit about that kind of community. We need to learn to talk about it in a way that illuminates the seriousness of those social relationships. Saying these relationships are serious begs the question, Who doesn't know that? Yet, I rarely hear anyone talk about the consequences of these relationships.

I think about Emily talking about her hope that students will learn to see the good in everybody. During our conversation, she has the time to think about this. I think to her surprise, she said she didn't really talk about that with her students. I also think about one of the students whom I interviewed after the cheating incident in my classroom. When I asked him if he had thought about saying something to his friends who cheated, he said no, but now thinking about it, he should have. My point with these examples is that it is often during a sustained conversation that we see where we have not given voice to our own ideas. We assume that relationships matter and we know that we experience conflicts in these relationships, but in schools we don't have many moments in our classes when we actually talk about this. Mary spoke of how wonderful it was when there was real give and take in her classroom, but said, almost wistfully, that it wasn't the daily pattern of interaction.

This is a fact of being human: We hold many assumptions and we don't always think about how we talk about and act on these assumptions. This is where reflective thinking comes in, for we need the time to say what we think, in order to see whether those ideas hold up outside of our heads. We need to see whether we say what we mean and mean what we say. The importance of making these ideas explicit allows us to judge our own ideas against the ideas of others. This judgment brings us to the way we teach teachers, both experienced teachers and those new to the work.

RELATIONSHIPS AND TEACHER EDUCATION

I believe that in both pre- and inservice education, we must include multiple conversations about what is moral and how morality fits into public education. I emphasize that when I define morality, I define it as paying attention to the interactions that we carry on. The interactions to which I refer are those with people we know well and, as important, with people with whom we are in temporary connection and even those whom we do not know well; we must emphasize the significance of these relationships for our students' cognitive and ethical growth.

Dewey (Parker, 1996) wrote, "Since education is a social process and there are many kinds of societies, a criterion for educational criticism and construction implies a *particular* social ideal" (p. 42, emphasis in original). He is not ignoring the idea that we take a stand when we talk of the kind of society we want, and he wants one in which there is free communication among all groups. "An undesirable society, in other words, is one which internally and externally sets up barriers to free intercourse and communication of experience" (p. 42).

Almost all discussions of a democratic society include the necessity of this free and open dialogue, and many books have been written on the topic of democratic education and the connection of that to a democratic society. "Such a society must have a type of education which gives individuals a personal interest in social relationships and the habits of mind which secure social changes without introducing disorder" (Dewey, in Parker, 1996, p. 42). The idea that Dewey points to is social relationships, and that is the idea that is missing from most of the conversation about education. I am suggesting that in order to teach in a democratic way, we must realize that social relationships must be developed, and developed in an explicit way.

We have seen several examples of the way that a relationship can impede honest dialogue. One might say those aren't real relationships, and I would agree, but to ignore the fact that we teach amid those relationships is to be blind to a serious difficulty in education. Many of our students will not take intellectual or ethical risks if they feel their relationships will be jeopardized. Many adults will follow the same pattern. Equally important, if a person, whether a student or an adult, does not develop responsibility for social relationships, it is far too easy to say, I did what is right and I am not responsible for any other person's actions. When do we develop the individual responsibility to take those risks? When does responsibility turn into doing something that is not one's business? Those are real questions and I don't know what the answers are, for there is not an easy template, an easy universal way to answer those questions. However, I do know that if we don't see those questions as embedded in the very fabric of the social relationships in which we all participate, we will continue to miss the point.

Parker (1996) worried that real democratic practices have remained outside of schools. He wrote that recognizing diversity is crucial to democracy, and while we talk of diversity, we don't actually practice democracy:

Curriculum planning that takes seriously this heterogeneity is not common. The mere provision of playgrounds, lunchrooms, gymnasiums, heterogeneous classrooms, and extracurricular activities falls short of the associationist vision of commonality *where within and among these settings problems of common living are identified and mutual deliberation and problem-solving activity is undertaken as a routine practice of school life.* Ironically, conflict resolution, "tolerating diversity," and even "multicultural education," often function as discourses of avoidance, encouraging school people mistakenly to act against conflict, muffling or preventing it or rushing to put it out when it flames up, rather than seizing upon it to nurture diversity while working out the practices of democratic living. They are not at odds. (p. 2, emphasis in original)

Parker quotes Dewey and writes himself about the lack of the kind of give and take that Mary described as so wonderful to watch in her classroom and something that her students wanted to do again. Yet, she described it as an unusual moment. If Parker is right that democracy isn't practiced much in our schools, perhaps it is because we haven't yet thought hard enough about how democracy is enacted in the context of social relationships and because we don't have "the habits of mind" that allow us to critique—to give and take—within that context. We have the habit of mind of winning, but do we have the habit of mind of attention?

CHANGING THE CULTURE OF SCHOOLING

Jerome Bruner (1996) wrote about the culture of education and worried that the very institution of schooling may get in the way of learners' scaffolding each other. He is talking about learning, but I would suggest that the culture of schooling may get in the way of learners' seeing themselves in relationship to one another. "Getting in the way" is that sense of fear described above. In order to change that, we must be more explicit about what is going on for not only our students but for us. If we were to construct a culture of relational education, we might refer to others (Gilligan, Noddings, Martin) who have described what could be called a culture of care. Those ideas as well as the ideas of democratic education are invaluable in constructing a culture of relational education. The idea of culture is an important one, for we would want to construct a culture of care and relationships and demonstrate that culture.

We would want to talk about what responsibility in relationship means, and more than just setting a rule such as, don't put anyone down, we would want to talk about what is the give and take of conflict in relationship. We would want to talk about how we learn to think about paying a kind of "just attention" (Murdoch, 1970, p. 34) to another's situation and argument. We would want to talk about not avoiding conflict, but learning from it, for "confrontation is a strong but risky medicine for unawareness." It is risky because it "is more likely to arouse anger and resentment than to raise consciousness" (Bruner, 1996, p. 148). So, we might want to talk about how to think about conflict as it exists in our democratic relationships. And we would want to learn to talk about relationships without having to say, "Is that too mushy?"

Bruner (1996) suggests we "need a surer sense of what to teach to whom and how to go about teaching it in such a way that it will make those taught more effective, less alienated, and better human beings. . . . What we need is a school reform movement with a better sense of where we are going, with deeper convictions about what kind of people we want to be" (p. 118). That sounds like Dewey's saying that we need to know the kind of society we want. The connection between the kind of society we want and the kind of education we want is crucial, and a critical part of that connection is the kind of social relationships we can develop.

We need to think about what kind of habits of mind we could develop to help us hold both the conflict and the comfort of relationships. For that I would return to the ideas of the moral orientations discussed in Chapter 2. The moral orientations provide two ways of looking both at the equality and equity necessary for relationships—the justice orientation—and at the response and attachment necessary in relationships—the care orientation. Gilligan (1988) described them as being like an ambiguous figure, the vase and the face, or the duck and the rabbit. You might be able to see one but not the other until you shift the figure ground. A lovely example of that is provided by Bruner (1996) and it is worth quoting in its entirety. He wrote:

> Niels Bohr once confessed the story of how he had arrived at the idea of complementarity in physics—illustrated, for example, by the principle that you cannot specify both the position and the velocity of a particle simultaneously and therefore you cannot include both in the same set of equations. The general idea had first struck him as a moral dilemma. His son had stolen a trinket from the local notions shop, but some days later, stricken with guilt, he had confessed the theft to his father. As Bohr put it, although he was greatly touched by this moral act of contrition, he was also mindful of his son's wrongdoing: "But I was struck by the fact that I could not think of

my son at the same moment both in the light of love and in the light of justice." (pp. 124–125)

These two moral orientations help us think about our moral responses in relationship. Thinking about both of them in connection to the ideas we have about social relationships in schools is a habit of mind we need to develop. The orientations are a necessity because they provide us with ideas that we can use to think about how to negotiate our social relationships as well as those relationships we might call intimate. The explicit acknowledgment that we are in relationship is also a necessity, for that acknowledgment opens us to our moral responsibility in those relationships.

SIX

Expanding Our Idea of Relationships

S CHOOLS EXIST in a particular context, a particular society. Children
learn within these contexts, and they learn what to value more by what
they observe than by what they are told to think. Within these particular
historical and personal contexts, meaning is created through the interaction between a child and her experience. When I think about the particular historical moment in which I am writing this book, I can feel despair; I
wonder how people of all ages, not just children, are creating meaning. I
read about the culture of meanness (Mills, 1997), the argument culture
(Tannen, 1998), and a society that has lost a sense of community (Bellah, 2004;
Putnam, 2000). Since I wrote my first article on cheating in 1991, former students, friends, and my mother have continued to send me newspaper clippings about cheating; in the past few years, there have been articles in the
Canton Repository (McManus, 1996), the *Hartford Current* (Stansbury, 1997),
the *Boston Globe* (Secor, 2004), and *The Nation* (Callahan, 2004) that state that
more students than ever are cheating.

There are articles that suggest the postgame handshake was dumped
because of the fights that occurred during that particular end-of-game
ritual, articles that say that young people like their TV mean, and numerous articles, both in papers and in more academic journals, about the rise
in bullying and the programs that are developed to deal with it. It seems
as if we are creating meaning in a culture that lacks any sense of community. We are out of relationship at many levels, and the work referenced
above deals only with the United States internally. The list would be much
longer and even more disturbing if articles about the United States and its
way of participating in the global community were included.

Writing about the death of the playwright Arthur Miller, another playwright, Tony Kushner (2005), wrote, "Arthur was a grieving pessimist, but
what truly progressive person isn't?" The idea of "grieving pessimist" resonated with me and I wonder where a "grieving pessimist" finds hope.
Again, Kushner's commentary is important: "[Miller] was his own prov-

ing ground; he felt his successes and his failures as a human being were consequential to something greater than himself, and so they were publicly examined and, in a sense, the only thing worth talking about. . . . *He wasn't certain that a single individual has relevance to our collective survival, but he saw no other question worth pursuing"* (pp. 6 and 8, emphasis added).

It would be extremely naive to suggest either that the articles referenced above represent the totality of our society, or that if we just all were friendlier, these headlines would disappear. It is not, however, naive to consider the importance of an individual and, more explicitly, the way the individual sees herself in relationship to known and unknown others. For this "grieving pessimist," there is "no other question worth pursuing."

DEVELOPING RELATIONSHIPS IN THE CLASSROOM

I have been arguing that it is critical to teach students the importance of their thinking about themselves not only as individuals but also as people thinking and acting in the context of the multiple dimensions of relationships in a classroom. In order for students of any age to learn about the dimensions of relationship examined in the previous chapters and the role they play in these relationships, they must learn three things:

1. How to pay attention to the language of the relationships in which we are all embedded.
2. How to listen to and imagine the other.
3. How to pay just attention to the other.

Among those who can teach this are teachers in the day-to-day work and conversation in a classroom. Teachers must, in fact, do this. We want schools to teach not only academic skills but also the skills students need in order to act as citizens in a complex world. The only way to do this is to teach actively how this is done.

Vygotsky (1978) and other learning theorists teach us that a wise adult or more competent peer is necessary to make sure that learning happens in the zone of proximal development. Vygotsky says by asking questions and providing opportunities to think, a teacher or more competent student can stretch a person to achieve more than the person might achieve on his or her own—what one can do with help today, one can do alone tomorrow. Therefore, if a teacher talks about the importance of relationships and works with a student modeling how to think about the relationships in a classroom community, the student ultimately will begin to think about these relationships on his or her own. We must be the more competent teacher about relationships, and to do that, we must recognize how important those relationships are for cognitive and ethical growth. We must be in the habit of thinking about these relationships and be explicit about their importance to the students we teach.

In the work on learning and teaching, there is ample evidence (for example, Hancock, 1999; Palincsar & Brown, 1986) that explicit teaching is necessary in order for students to really understand material. I am not arguing for an explicit curriculum like character education or the older curricula on values education. Instead, I am arguing that the language of relationships should be an explicit language in our schools. May said that she assumes nothing about what the children know. She teaches them what she wants them to know and explicitly how she wants them to behave. Lesley said she explicitly teaches her students empathy and what that means in action. These teachers are not discussing a curriculum to be tested, but an often-hidden curriculum that should be uncovered. We need to use the words that the teachers in this study used and teach them to our students. The language of classroom relationships is not limited to the dimensions of relationships described in this book, but they are parts of it and they are part of a curriculum that must be dealt with in our classrooms.

Teaching the Language of Relationships

Teacher education programs have become increasingly more rigorous in terms of preparation, especially in liberal arts courses. Professional development programs for inservice teachers are already full of work on meeting standards and keeping up with new technology. There isn't much room in either of these teacher education sites for courses on the language of relationships. There wouldn't be room in a classroom for this kind of work either, and frankly none of these venues would be appropriate. We need to make this language not part of a course, but part of our lives, a habit of thinking. We do this by asking our students and ourselves not only what the consequences of our actions are for others, as Selman (2003) would have us do, but also how we are acting *in this relationship*. Am I acting like I am in a relationship and am a responsible actor in that relationship? What words would I use to describe how I am acting and what my goals are? This is where the language of relationships becomes critical. It is one thing to say the consequences of my actions are that Sam is angry; that makes me focus on Sam. It is another thing to say he is angry because he thinks I was unfair or I was not caring. Then the focus becomes on both of us and our relationship.

Those who teach teachers, and teachers already in the classroom, must work to develop this habit of mind. We must work to teach our students to "think against the grain" (Cochran-Smith, 1991) and to critique the current focus on individualism. This is crucial because the current focus in our society and schools is on the individual and how that individual feels and what she achieves, rather than on any connection she has to the lives immediately around her and those that are further removed from her. Gloria Ladson-Billings (1994) calls this focus on the individual and on that individual's achievement "competitive individualism" (p. 69).

Josselson (1992) worries about the same issue when she writes:

> Sociologists and cultural critics are increasingly alarmed by the radical individualism of American culture and the concomitant overvaluation of the self. . . . The centrality of the self in modern psychology is both cause and consequence of this cultural tilt. By glorifying selfhood and individual enterprise, psychology has both absorbed American values and encourages a social philosophy that puts the interests of the self at the helm. As a result, the current dominant psychological narrative of human development is a tale of human beings set adrift from each other, pursuing their course of "autonomy" and "independence." Thus psychology joins the culture of narcissism in shared idolatry of the self, bestowing praise on self-reliance, self-expression, self-awareness, and self-fulfillment. And in paying such homage, both our culture and our psychology deny our essential dependence on each other. (p. 12)

It is no wonder that schools also focus on this individualism to the detriment of a focus on the self in relationship. It is not that the focus of school should be either on the individual or on the individual in relationship, but the focus must be on both. It is our obligation, and I would say it is a moral obligation, to teach our students that their identities are firmly rooted in both places. In order to teach our students both aspects of their selves, teachers must talk about relationships explicitly. In Chapter 4 Emily talks about how important it is for her to have her students see that there is something worthwhile in each of their fellow classmates. She calls it "seeing the good in everyone." As we talked about it, Emily realized that perhaps she had not been explicit enough about that with her students and said she was going to talk about that idea more clearly. If we value relationships, our beliefs about what we should do in those relationships seem so obvious to us that we assume everyone has the same ideas. We should not assume that our students think about their being responsible to and for one another. We need to explicitly express that idea in our classroom language.

Developing the Ability to Listen and to Imagine the Other

We must be explicit about the language of relationships. We also must develop our imaginations so that we can imagine other people's experiences. This is done through art, music, and literature, as Maxine Greene (1995) argues. It also is done concretely by asking the questions suggested by the work of Selman (2003) and Damon (1988) and others who ask questions about how the other feels. I suggest it also is done by listening to what others say. Mary described a wonderful moment in her class when her students were talking about their response to a book. They really listened to one another and she was thrilled; she said it didn't happen often, but when it did, it was wonderful.

Listening to one another takes courage because we might hear something we don't want to hear. This presents a real difficulty for us. Each of the teachers I spoke with has rules about what is okay to say in class, and what is not (no put-downs, no mean things). Of course, we need these rules to avoid gratuitous put-downs and comments that are meant to be cool, not kind. But how do we learn to say things that are hard to say or hard to hear? In my own classes, I can feel uncomfortable when a student says something that could cause another student pain. I worry about how to protect students from what others might say, while at the same time I want to make sure that ideas and opinions are aired, so they can be examined. It takes skill to lead a discussion in which multiple views are expressed; it also takes courage.

It takes courage to even stop and have a discussion. There is so much content to cover, so much to attend to in a class that sometimes even stopping for a conversation requires a kind of resolve. Discussions aren't neat; questions get asked and not answered. Ideas get put out and not followed up on; other ideas take us to places we didn't expect to go. A student once said that discussions sometimes feel like tossing a Nerf ball around—you never know where it is going to end and whether the ending will be coherent and satisfactory. There must be trust in a classroom to follow a discussion and to allow for the ambiguity that is often part of a discussion. It also takes trust to suspend judgment when something is said that is unexpected or painful. We may have to learn to believe what Piaget believed—that there is a logic to the way people make sense of their world. In order for students to develop this trust and the courage to listen, relationships in the classroom community must be acknowledged.

Fine and Weis (2003) present classrooms in which students and teachers have discussions and learn about one another's views—and this learning is often painful. Fine discusses a classroom teacher's and her own response to students who are talking in ways that are not just and that are painful for the adults to hear. What is interesting about this discussion is that the teachers and the students stick with one another. Fine does not explicitly use the word *relationship* to describe their sticking with one another, but I would argue that the relationships of trust, respect, and fairness, in the sense of letting everyone have their voice, were the reason they did stick it out and listen to one another, even as the speakers changed their minds. Fine and Weis also describe an African American young man who kept quiet for most of the class discussions: He felt that nobody "would catch his back" (p. 131). He speaks for many students who don't feel supported by the relationships in a classroom and, because of that lack of trust, never say what is on their minds. These relationships work in ways that give some people voice and silence others.

Discussions also can be viewed in negative ways by those observing a classroom. Emily described how in her effort to give everyone a voice, the discussions in her class often went on for some time. An administrative observer told her that she often went on too long. Perhaps she did, but how else will students learn what someone else thinks unless everyone who wants to gets a chance to speak?

Discussions can be thought of as unfruitful if they are compared to throwing a Nerf ball, as the student previously quoted judged them. They can be scary and silence some students, like the student Fine and Weis describe. Sometimes they are both of these things; however, they are important educational opportunities for learning how to express ideas and talk across differences. It is obvious that one doesn't know how discussions will end until they end, but the end of a discussion is not always obvious. Sometimes what is said remains in a student's mind beyond the classroom period, semester, or even year. That possibility is the result of really listening and thinking. That learning and thinking are more real to me than a score on a test, but they present great difficulty in schools that are judged on achievement scores. It is hard to test learning that takes hold days, weeks, or even months after a classroom period.

Leading discussions, then, takes courage and the will to hear one another out. Dialogue and discussion, however, are ways to know another and hear other views; they may be the only ways to do this. These dialogues and discussions occur in the context of relationships in classrooms. "We come to know others via the same avenues we know ourselves: acting in public, speaking in public" (Plotz, 1999, p. B45), and through serious discussion.

Listening to others and their ideas is the place where we can begin to hear different views from our own; it seems obvious, but this hearing of other voices allows us to know not in the abstract, but very concretely that there are other ways to see things that are different from our way. Once we know how the voices of others sound and what their ideas are, we can begin to imagine their voices when they aren't there. Requiring students to do this and helping them understand why it is important is crucial; this is an interruption in the fast-paced, individualistic culture in which they live. As they listen to other concrete voices, we can begin to ask students for other ways to see an issue and how someone else would see a problem; this gives them the space to imagine alternative answers.

Some would argue that alternative answers and many voices lead to a relativistic conception of cognitive and ethical issues, but I would argue just the opposite. William Perry's (1981) work is useful here, for he discusses what it means to know multiple perspectives on problems and ideas and then to evaluate these perspectives and arrive at a solution that is "tentative but wholehearted" (p. 79). This is what an adult must do: evaluate different perspectives, weigh the evidence, and then come to a commitment. Perry writes that the solution is wholehearted because we believe it and commit to it, but tentative because if we are willing to keep our minds open, we could learn something that would cause us to reevaluate our commitment.

Younger students are not often required to make the kind of commitments that mature adults must make, but they must learn to imagine alternative solutions to problems and then to decide which they think is the best solution. Children as young as 6 did this in the fable study. This kind of thinking prepares them for two things. The first is cognitive and is described by Kagan (1984), who wrote that children must be encouraged to think critically and solve problems by thinking of a variety of solutions and then helped to make decisions about which alternative is best. The second is ethical—imagining different points of views in a situation gives even young children the realization that their perspective is not the only one.

Learning to Pay Attention

Finally, listening and imagining are not enough; we must pay attention to others. Nel Noddings (1999) writes that a person for whom care is shown must feel cared for in order for the act of caring to matter. How do we know if another feels cared for unless we pay attention to the person and not just our intention?

We must pay enough attention to another person to try to figure out what he or she thinks. Iris Murdoch (1970), building on the work of Simone Weil, calls this an act of "just attention"—the act of directing "a just and loving gaze at a specific situation" (p. 32). She writes about the importance of just attention in solving moral problems, for if we pay just attention we can understand a situation (or problem) and then perhaps be directed to solve the dilemma. She, however, also suggests that we often cannot solve a dilemma even when we have taken the time to pay just attention. Her view requires us to be humble about what we know and can understand. In my view, we need to pay attention to others and to their specific situations in order to begin to confront both our differences and our common purposes—in bigger terms, our humanity.

If we pay attention, we may begin to enter a dialogue with "an other." This dialogue may be either a concrete conversation or an imagined one. In either case, the dialogue can uncover the dimensions of the relationship in which we are located. This dialogue is one that should not be only in our terms, but that won't ever be perfectly in the other person's terms either. It is this lack of clarity and finality to which I am drawn. This is the dilemma of living with others; we are incapable of perfect understanding. Relationship is a process never completed. When we think we know someone, or about someone, we are bound to be surprised. How do we learn to absorb this tension—this sense of incompleteness? I would say it is one of the "challenges to care" (Noddings, 1992) that schools should take up, but not in a standardized curriculum.

While some might find the various character development resources useful, I don't believe this is where we need to focus our energy and our time. Rather, the challenge to care is taught explicitly by the language the teacher uses and in the conversations the teacher has with her students. It is not a lesson a day or a value a week, but is embedded in the ordinary day-to-day talk in a classroom.

This is where the idea of "teaching against the grain" (Cochran-Smith, 1991) fits. Teachers must learn to slow down and take the risk of discussing relationships explicitly with their students. They must work against the fast pace of the day-to-day lesson, of the work that must be done before the end of the period or the end of the term. This is not done by replacing or discarding traditional lesson plans; it is done by paying attention to how students interact with one another and by asking questions and naming explicitly the kind of interactions observed. It means developing a habit of thinking about relationships and community, and taking a moment to label the relationships seen in the classroom.

If the power of relationships is something that teachers think about and plan for in their classrooms, there is the potential to teach students the moral implications of those relationships. We can be clear about the dimensions of relationships in our classrooms and can begin to uncover the responsibilities we have to those in the wider communities in which we act and live. There is a connection between the relationships developed in a classroom and the bigger issues we face in society.

COMMUNITY IN THE CLASSROOM

In 2000, Laurel Thatcher Ulrich gave a keynote address at a conference titled Women Writing, Writing Women in Portland, Maine. She said that Americans had lost most of their public spaces and their sense of community. She used the example that historically people gathered to celebrate events like July 4th. This coming together gave people a sense of belonging to a group bigger than their family and developed a sense of community and a sense of a public space.

More recently, the same argument was made by Roberta Brandes-Gratz and Stephen A. Goldsmith (2005). Writing about the recent Central Park installation by Christo and his wife Jeanne-Claude, they argued:

> The public's enthusiastic embrace of this populist spectacle should be a wake-up call across the country. For too long, communities have been losing public spaces that offer the opportunity for people to serendipitously mix, mingle and meet. Today, the privately owned mall is often a community's only remaining

gathering space. Unlike in a true public place, public assembly or leaflet distribution can be legally denied in private malls. And when genuine public places are absent, the human hunger for connection is fulfilled by "hanging out" at the Wal-Mart or roaming the corridors of any big box. (p. 25)

If we are truly bowling alone, as Putnam (2000) would have it, or we have lost a sense of community and many of our public spaces, then we must think hard about the public spaces that remain. School is one of those remaining spaces. Even as vouchers, privatization, and some aspects of charter schools are eroding the public in schools and even as the public in the schools has been resegregated (Orfield, Eaton, and Harvard Project on School Desegregation, 1996), our schools remain one of the last truly public spaces in the United States. It is in schools, then, that we must learn our responsibilities in relationship and learn the way we must think and act to build relationships and to build a community where we are responsible to and for one another and where we can hear one another across diffferences.

We have learned to go it alone, to depend on ourselves, and to relegate our concern and our care to those we know. I agree with Parker Palmer (1998), who wrote, "We lose our capacity to entertain people and ideas that are alien to what we think and who we are. The therapeutic model exploits our fear of otherness by reducing community to whatever can take familial or friendly form" (p. 91). Community cannot be reduced to those who are our family and our friends. The term *community* also should not be applied to a classroom if those in the class are not communicating their similarities and their differences, and are not really paying attention to the others in that community. Community means acknowledging that we are in relationship with one another.

While we may acknowledge community in classrooms, it may not be labeled as a relationship. It is the acknowledgment of the relationship that opens us to our responsibilities in the relationship. We must reinvigorate a sense of community by seriously discussing what responsibilities we have in communities— both those communities we can know and those we do not. To learn about our responsibilities in a variety of communities, it is necessary to understand community not as an abstract theoretical construct, but to see ourselves in concrete relationships in those communities. Understanding responsibilities in communities will not automatically reduce the incidents of cheating, bullying, or rude behavior, but it gives us a place to ask the question, What are the consequences of my actions on the people in this community? Classrooms are the concrete communities in which we can learn about these responsibilities; they are laboratories of community.

Public schools are public spaces, and public spaces mean that the people and ideas discussed inside those spaces are not homogeneous. The need for a place "to leaflet," described in the quote above, is a metaphor for the need for schools to be a place for handing out and evaluating differences, both different people and different ideas. That will not happen when people, like the boy described by Fine and Weis, are worried that "no one will get their back." You don't have to be a friend to get someone's back, nor do you have to have the same ideas; however, you must understand your relationship to that other person and the responsibilities in that relationship. Those responsibilities are captured in the dimensions of relationships that have been discussed, and those dimensions must be articulated in order for a community of relationships to function.

If we make the power of relationships something that teachers think about and plan for, and talk about in their classrooms, there is the potential to teach students the moral implications of those relationships. We can be clear about the dimensions of relationships in our classrooms and we can begin to uncover the responsibilities we have to those in the wider communities in which we act and live. One can't explore these ideas through a set curriculum, but one can explore them by keeping the power of relationships as a central category in teachers' thinking and by supporting teachers as they work on ways to both talk about this and develop relationships with their students. We can't dismiss this kind of talk as "garbage," as Chris worried it might sound like. We can't dismiss it as not important in schools, for while we focus on student achievement, we also must focus on student interactions and on building relationships in our classrooms. While the relationships that children have with one another might not be long lasting and intimate, they can be practice for seeing the self in relationship to others and for seeing the responsibilities that one has to others. The faces of those with whom we build relationships in the classroom are concrete, and the practice of feeling responsible for those concrete individuals, if made explicit and valuable, has the potential to make us feel responsible for those we don't know. If Vygotsky is right and our external world becomes internalized, then the external acknowledgment that we participate in relationships in classrooms, and that those relationships build community, has the potential to become internalized and change the way we think about ourselves in the world.

RELATIONSHIPS OUTSIDE THE CLASSROOM

The connection between classroom relationships and social justice has not been addressed explicitly, and that connection may be a key in learning how to be responsible citizens in a world that has been described by David Halberstam (2005), among others, as one "with a much lower level of basic civility" than that of even 50 years ago (p. 18). There is not an automatic transfer from seeing oneself as in relationships with intimates to seeing oneself in relationship to those who are not known to us; however, seeing oneself as located in many relationships holds a promise for doing so. That promise is connected to seeing that one is responsible in relationship to unknown others. This responsibility has the potential to prepare our students to care about and work for social justice.

It is fairly obvious that we can learn to care for and try to treat fairly the people with whom we come in daily contact, but how do we learn to care for those people who appear as abstractions in our world—those whom Maxine Greene (1988) calls "unknown others" and whom Brian Hehir (2005) describes as people at "the edge of the circle of life"? Is it possible to think about oneself in relationship to those unknown others?

Several years ago when I taught *The Dialectic of Freedom* (Greene, 1988), my students had trouble with the concept of "unknown others." They were younger students, 1st- and 2nd-year college students, who found this concept baffling. It wasn't that they closed their minds to thinking about humanity in the abstract; in fact, they regularly spoke about humanity and the role that society plays in all of our lives. They simply were unable to get a handle on the concept that people who were not known to them had any link to their lives. They were unable to *imagine* those unknown others as people for whom they were responsible, let alone as people whose freedom was connected to theirs. At that time, I was unable to help them do that, much to my dismay as a teacher.

Several years later, after the tragedy of September 11, 2001, I had a similar experience, with a slightly different outcome. When the planes hit New York, Washington, DC, and Pennsylvania, many Colgate students were directly affected. Alumni of the college were killed and students lost loved ones. The university canceled classes and devoted a day to our consideration of this. The following day classes resumed and most of us who had classes that day weren't quite sure what to do when we actually met our students again. I was teaching a class about teaching and learning to upper-level students. I assigned them an essay by Eleanor Duckworth, "Making Sure Everyone Gets Home Safely" (1996). I wanted them to think about their responsibilities as teachers when something this catastrophic happened, and I thought this essay would help us do that, but I wasn't certain where our discussion would take us.

In class we began to talk about the tragedy and about the various ways that public schools that we knew about had responded. We talked about what schools' and teachers' responsibilities were in horrific situations and in less dramatic day-to-day situations. As our discussion continued, I asked my students what children they felt responsible for, and their answers were predictable in the way that responsibility often is conceived. They said they were responsible for the children they knew, the children they might have, and the children they would teach. I asked them if they felt responsibility for the children in Madison County, the county in which Colgate is located. There was a long period of silence in the room and then one of the students I liked a great deal had the courage to say no. I asked why and she said that she didn't share their community, even though she lived in it. Because I was working on the ideas in this book, I pressed the class a bit more about relationships, and they were honest in the way they limited their ideas about whom they were in relationship to. Their views were much like the views that Josselson critiqued (see Chapter 5). This was an important moment for all of us. I believe some of my students began to think about their responsibilities in a broader way, and I continued to think about the potential of imagining the self in relationships.

The student above saw the children in Madison County every day. She was and I am sure remains committed to social justice ideas, but had not yet been able to make the connection between her abstract commitment to social justice and the concrete lives of children she didn't know. This is similar to the way that Adrienne Rich describes Mary Chesnut (Rich, 1978). Chesnut was committed to the abolition of slavery, but when she was confronted with a Black woman slave, she didn't react. Rich writes that Chesnut could not imagine their lives as connected. This lack of connection prevented Chesnut from feeling real responsibility for the woman, even as she abominated slavery. Rich found that discomforting and so do I.

Certainly just imagining how lives across this country and indeed around the globe are connected is not going to move the students we teach or even ourselves to act in socially just ways. But without that imagining, I am quite certain we can lose sight too easily of the importance of acting in ways that promote social justice. Certainly, seeing ourselves in relationship in our temporary communities won't teach us to see ourselves in relationship to larger, more abstract communities. However, without the concrete understanding that we are connected and responsible in community, we focus too easily on ourselves. How does, for example, an economically well off White suburban girl learn to "care for" a homeless Black urban woman and perhaps learn that some of the choices she makes as a person of economic privilege have consequences for the urban poor? How does that girl learn to see herself in connection to that woman? Can we be concerned about social justice if we can't imagine the faces of folks who aren't like us and if we can't see how our lives affect theirs? If we think only that we have not been directly responsible for injustice, then can we see how our unearned privilege perpetuates the kind of thinking that might perpetuate those injustices? I don't think we can understand that unless we begin very concretely to teach children to see others as part of their lives and themselves as part of others' lives.

I am not interested in a simple-minded, sentimental argument about just getting along. Seeing ourselves in relationship to others demands hard cognitive and emotional work, and, in fact, getting along is not the goal. Getting along can be done without any work; just think about all the clichés that describe this: go along to get along, don't rock the boat, and so on. Being in the kind of relationship I am describing is about not going along to get along but listening and working to understand others, especially the differences among people. Understanding how we differ from others in experiences, beliefs, and the ways we know our worlds is the first step in understanding how we can work together productively across our differences.

In "Human Personality," Simone Weil argues that "in an unstable society the privileged have a bad conscience," and choose not to hear what she calls "the afflicted" (Panichas, 1977, p. 326). She writes that those who lack privilege are unheard by those who have privilege because "affliction is by nature inarticulate" and those who are privileged put "distance" between themselves and those without privilege "at the first possible moment." She argues that it is natural to avoid thinking about and acknowledging those who, in her terms, are "afflicted" (p. 327). If I interpret her essay correctly, she goes on to acknowledge that language is powerful because it "formulates opinions," but says that language also can be dangerous because "at the very best, a mind enclosed in language is in prison" (p. 330).

While language can be a prison, it is not always. It also provides a different kind of space; it may provide an opening for a different way of thinking. The language of relationships has the power to articulate the many responsibilities we have in relationships and has the potential to teach us those responsibilities in connection to those without privilege in our world. We must start where we can, which is in the classroom by teaching our students that they are in relationship to one another and pointing out what they owe one another because of those relationships. They owe each other fairness, respect, care, and empathy in the context of the part of their lives they spend together. Then we must work to stretch our students cognitively and ethically to imagine the relationships they are in with others in the world outside of their classrooms—to hear the afflicted near and far and then to imagine what their responsibilities are to them.

Schrader (1999) argues that students are not taught to analyze moral issues nor are they taught to analyze relational issues. Selman (2003) argues that it is imperative to make seeing the consequences of our actions second nature. Yet, we can't care about consequences if we don't care about those who suffer them. Learning to analyze both moral and relational issues and to see the consequences of our actions must be embedded in existing relationships, and part of the purpose of education must be to start learning this.

The purpose of education has been narrowed in many ways to a focus on achievement, yet there are constant calls for questioning of this narrow purpose (Johnston & Ross, 2001). Eisner (2003) writes:

> The function of schools is surely not primarily to enable students to do well on tests—or even to do well in school itself. What one wants, it seems to me is to provide a curriculum and a school environment that enable students to develop the dispositions, the appetites, the skills, and the ideas that will allow them to live personally satisfying *and socially productive lives*. (p. 651, emphasis added)

In order to live socially productive lives, we have to see ourselves as part of a social group, a community, a society. That seems so obvious as to be banal, but we constantly speak of society as if we aren't a part of it. Think of all the times we say or hear, well society is _____ ; you can fill in the blank. That language puts us apart from society, not embedded in it.

Schools must teach us to see ourselves as part of society and to see that society as something that can be made better. Education has long been understood as an avenue to social justice (Rury, 2002). Adair (2001) argues we must "take a step toward ensuring that education remains a truly democratic project that has the potential for enacting social change and fostering economic equity" (p. 237).

Those of us who struggle to work toward social justice (Cochran-Smith, 2004; Darling-Hammond, French, & Garcia Lopez, 2002) understand that, indeed, our society and the world in which we live must be made better. Race is still an unresolved dilemma in our country and globally. We have children who are uninsured and who don't have enough to eat in the richest country in the world. We judge people by their religion and live in a world where terror attacks are the focus of the nightly news. And most recently as I write, there is the tragic, disorganized, and racist response to those displaced by Hurricane Katrina. There is, indeed, much to be done.

Noddings (1992, 2002) has argued that schools should help students find their best selves and then move those best selves outward into society. At whatever level we teach, we as teachers must work to help each of our students find his or her best self, and we must work to explicitly teach that an aspect of finding our best selves is finding where we stand in relationship. These relationships are obviously with those we love, but also and less obviously with those we know only slightly, or not at all—in other words, relationships with those with whom we live in community.

In teaching this, we are not teaching students to be nice to one another. We are doing something much more important and much more difficult to do—we are teaching students to think critically about who they are in a complicated world.

In writing about teaching her students to think, Elizabeth Minnich (2003) writes that thinking "is exploratory, suggestive; it does not prove anything, or finally arrive anywhere" (p. 20). She does not dismiss rational deliberation or knowledge as unimportant, but argues that we as teachers need to do more than teach our students to deliberate rationally and absorb knowledge. We must teach our students to think; she connects this way of thinking to morality because if we learn to think, we can stay open to people who are different from us.

> Thus, to say people are thoughtful or thought provoking suggests that they are open-minded, reflective, challenging—that they are more likely to question than to assert, inclined to listen to many sides, capable of making sensitive distinctions that hold differences in play rather than dividing in order to exclude, and desirous of persuading others rather than reducing them to silence by refuting them. (p. 20)

Her description of thinking takes her to a description of the way she wants her students to react to others. That way incorporates two of the ideas presented earlier; students who are thinkers in the way Minnich describes pay attention to others and listen carefully. We as teachers must teach them to do this. We also must teach them that when they listen to others, they must attend to the relationships in which they participate when they are listening. These relationships have obligations, and those obligations are expressed concretely by the language of relationships.

We have some tools to help us teach students about community, but unless we know why creating a classroom community is important even beyond the classroom, these tools produce only habits of action, not habits of mind. It is a habit of mind that must be developed. We must think habitually about how what we do has an impact on others. We must see ourselves in relationships with others and see the consequences of those relationships as moral consequences. Gilligan (1982) exposed a danger in thinking only of others, and that is not a danger I would want to replicate in classrooms; however, there is also a danger in not thinking of others. This tension of thinking of the self and others must be brought explicitly into the conversations in our schools.

We must pay close attention to ourselves as members of a community in which honest discussion can take place. Larry Blum (1997) argues that "attention to creating such community deserves attention as a distinct goal," for community is a place where both antiracist ideas and multicultural respect can be nurtured (p. 18). This is only one of the differences that can be better understood if we create a community of relationships where if trust can't be found, then fairness can be. Setting a goal of attending to community in a classroom, and then understanding the range of differences in that community, requires hard work, but it has the potential to move outward into imagining the differences found in the widening circles of community in which we are located.

In an article about higher education, Robert Bellah (2004) wrote, "A deep concern for justice and the common good as part of one's character is not an add-on that can be attained from a one-shot course in ethics. Rather it is a matter of what has traditionally been called formation" (p. 31). He goes on to make an argument he has made before and that is echoed in some of the ideas discussed earlier.

> Americans are sharply limited [in both cognitive knowledge and moral insight into the world]. Our central tradition makes us think of justice only in terms of individual rights and . . . we have little understanding of the common good. (p. 37)

The purpose of education must be to give us cognitive knowledge of ourselves and our world, but it also must give us moral insight into that world. That moral insight will come not from people trying to shape our moral beliefs or our family values, but from the kind of education that teaches us to think deeply, to be open to ideas and people, and to see ourselves in relationship to others—both those we know and those we can only imagine. This can be done only if we work together and ask, With whom am I in relationship? We can ask those questions only if we understand the multiple dimensions of relationship, and we can understand those multiple dimensions only if we talk about them, if we map the language of classroom relationships and then map that language onto the relationships we have in the wider world.

The purpose of this book has been to begin a conversation to map those relationships. It began as a conversation among six teachers and me and between scholars in psychology, philosophy, and education. As others read these ideas, they will add complexity to the work begun here. It is our obligation as educators to articulate that complexity to our students and to a wider community. This will, at the very least, highlight this concern in the public conversation about education—a conversation that is politicized and narrowly focused, and needs to be refocused. And although some would say this is too idealistic, articulating that complexity also has the potential to teach our students their responsibility to others in their world. Understanding that responsibility is the beginning of working toward a common good and a world that is more socially just.

References

Adair, V. C. (2001). Poverty and the (broken promise) of higher education. *Harvard Educational Review, 71*(2), 217–238.

Bellah, R. N. (2004). Education for justice and the common good. *Conversations on Jesuit Higher Education, 25,* 28–37.

Bellah, R. N., Madsen, R., Sullivan W. M., Swidler, A., & Tipton, S. M. (1985). *Habits of the heart.* Berkeley and Los Angeles: University of California Press.

Blum, L. (1997). Multicultural education as values education. Working papers. Harvard Project on Schooling and Children, pp. 1–34.

Brandes-Gratz, R., & Goldsmith, S. A. (2005, March 28). In the park with Christo. *The Nation, 280*(12), 25.

Brown, L., Argyris, D., Attanucci, J., Bardige, B., Gilligan, C., Johnston, K., Miller, B., Osborne, R., Tappan, M., Ward, J., & Wilcox, D. (1987). A guide to reading narratives of moral conflict and choice for self and moral voice. Unpublished manuscript, Harvard Graduate School of Education, Cambridge, MA.

Bruner, J. (1996). *The culture of education.* Cambridge, MA: Harvard University Press.

Callahan, D. (2004, February 9). Take back values. *The Nation,* 14–20.

Charney, R. S. (2002). *Teaching children to care.* Portland, ME: Stenhouse Press.

Cochran-Smith, M. (1991). Learning to teach against the grain. *Harvard Educational Review, 51*(3), 279–310.

Cochran-Smith. M. (2004). *Walking the road.* New York: Teachers College Press.

Connelly, F. M., & Clandinin, D. J. (1988). *Teachers as curriculum planners.* New York: Teachers College Press.

Damon, W. (1988). *The caring child.* New York: The Free Press.

Darling-Hammond, L., French, J., & Garcia Lopez, S. P. (2002). *Learning to teach for social justice.* New York: Teachers College Press.

Delpit, L. (1995). *Teaching other people's children.* New York: New Press.

Donaldson, M. (1978). *Children's minds.* New York: Norton.

Duckworth, E. (1996). *The having of wonderful ideas.* New York: Teachers College Press.

Eisner, E. (2003, May). Questionable assumptions about schooling. *Phi Delta Kappan, 84*(9), 648–657.

Fine, M., & Weis, L. (2003). *Silenced voices and extraordinary conversations*. New York: Teachers College Press.

Garrod, A. (Ed.). (1992). *Learning for life: Moral education theory and practice*. Westport, CT: Praeger.

Gilligan, C. (1977). In a different voice: Women's conceptions of self and morality. *Harvard Educational Review, 47,* 481–517.

Gilligan, C. (1982*). In a different voice: Psychological theory and women's development.* Cambridge, MA: Harvard University Press.

Gilligan, C. (1988). Adolescent development reconsidered. In C. Gilligan, J. V. Ward, & J. Taylor, (Eds.), *Mapping the moral domain: A contribution of women's thinking to psychology and research* (pp. vii–xxxix). Cambridge, MA: Harvard University Press.

Gilligan, C. (2000, February). *In a different voice—18 years later*. Paper presented at Colgate University, Hamilton, NY.

Gilligan, C., & Attanucci, J. (1988). Two moral orientations. *Merrill Palmer Quarterly, 34,* 223–237.

Gilligan, C., Langdale, S., Lyons, N., & Murphy, J. (1982). *The contributions of women's thought to developmental theory: The elimination of sex bias in moral development research and education* (Final Report to the National Institute of Education). Cambridge, MA.: Harvard University Press.

Gilligan, C., Ward, J. V., & Taylor, J. (Eds.). (1988). *Mapping the moral domain: A contribution of women's thinking to psychology and research*. Cambridge, MA: Harvard University Press.

Greene, M. (1988). *The dialectic of freedom*. New York: Teachers College Press.

Greene, M. (1995). *Releasing the imagination*. San Francisco: Jossey-Bass.

Grumet, M. (1988). *Bitter milk*. Amherst: University of Massachusetts Press.

Halberstam, D. (2005). A modest generation. *Harvard Magazine, 107*(5), 16–18.

Hancock, J. H. (1999). *The explicit teaching of reading*. Newark, DE: International Reading Association.

Hargreaves, A. (1992). Cultures of teaching. In A. Hargreaves & M. Fullan (Eds.), *Understanding teacher development* (pp. 216–240). New York: Teachers College Press.

Hehir, J. B. (2005, May). *Religion and politics: A new intensity and new complexity*. Baccalaureate address given at the One Hundred Eighty-Fourth Commencement, Colgate University, Hamilton, NY.

Hollingsworth, S. (1994). *Teacher research and urban literacy education*. New York: Teachers College Press.

Jackson, P. W. (1992). *Untaught lesson*. New York: Teachers College Press.

Johnson, S. M., Birkeland, S., Kardos, S. M., Kauffman, D., Liu, E., & Peske, H. G. (2001). *Retaining the next generation of teachers: The importance of school-based support*. Retrieved August 31, 2001, from http://www.edletter.org.

Johnston, D. K. (1985). *Two moral orientations, two problem-solving strategies: Adolescents' solutions to dilemmas in fables*. Unpublished doctoral dissertation, Harvard Graduate School of Education, Cambridge, MA.

Johnston, D. K. (1988). Adolescents' solutions to dilemmas in fables: Two moral orientations—two problem solving strategies. In C. Gilligan, J. V. Ward, & J. Taylor (Eds.), *Mapping the moral domain: A contribution of women's thinking to psychology and research* (pp. 49–71). Cambridge, MA: Harvard University Press.

Johnston, D. K. (1991). A story of cheating: Reflections on a moral dilemma. *Journal of Moral Education, 20*(3), 283–291.

Johnston, D. K. (1996). Cheating: The limits of individual integrity. *Journal of Moral Education, 25*(2), 159–171.

Johnston, D. K., Brown, L. M., & Christopherson, S. (1990). Adolescents' moral dilemmas: The context. *Journal of Youth and Adolescence, 19*, 615–623.

Johnston, D. K., & Maurer, M. (2002). Teaching and risk: Doing and undoing Shakespeare. In P. Skrebels & S. van der Hoeven (Eds.), *For all time: Critical issues in teaching Shakespeare* (pp. 100–111). Kent Town, South Australia: Wakefield Press.

Johnston, K., & Ross, H. (2001, August 13). Teaching to higher standards—from managing to imagining the purposes of education. *TCRecord.Org*.

Josselson, R. (1992). *The space between us—exploring the dimensions of human relationships*. San Francisco: Jossey-Bass.

Kagan, J. (1984). *The nature of the child*. New York: Basic Books.

Kegan, R. (1994). *In over our heads: The mental demands of modern life*. Cambridge, MA: Harvard University Press.

Kohlberg, L. (1948). From beds to bananas. *The Menorah Journal, 36*, 385–399.

Kohlberg, L. (1969). Stage sequence: The cognitive-developmental approach to socialization. In D. Goslin (Ed.), *Handbook of socialization theory and research* (pp. 347–481). New York: Rand McNally.

Kohlberg, L. (1976). Moral stages and moralization. In T. Lickona (Ed.), *Moral development and behavior* (pp. 31–54). New York: Holt, Rinehart and Winston.

Kohlberg, L., Levine, C., & Hewer, A. (1984). The current formulation of the theory. In L. Kohlberg (Ed.), *The psychology of moral development: Essays on moral development* Vol. 2 (pp. 212–320). San Francisco: Harper & Row.

Kohlberg, L. (with Mayer, R.). (1981). Development as the aim of education: The Dewey view. In L. Kohlberg (Ed.), *The philosophy of moral development: Moral stages and the idea of justice* (pp. 49–97). San Francisco: Harper & Row.

Kushner, T. (2005, June 13). Kushner on Miller. *The Nation, 280*(23), 6, 8.

Ladson-Billings, G. (1994). *The dreamkeepers*. San Francisco: Jossey-Bass.

Langdale, S. (1983). *Moral orientations and moral development: The analysis of care and justice reasoning across different dilemmas in females and males from childhood through adulthood.* Unpublished doctoral dissertation, Harvard Graduate School of Education, Cambridge, MA.

Lawrence-Lightfoot, S. (Producer). (1988). *A world of ideas with Bill Moyers* [Videotape]. New York and Chicago: Public Broadcasting Service.

Lifton, P. (1985). Individual differences in moral development: The relation of sex, gender, and personality to morality. *Journal of Personality* [Special issue], *53*(2), 306–334.

Lyons, N. (1983). Two perspectives: On self, relationships and morality. *Harvard Educational Review, 53*(2), 125–145.

Martin, J. R. (1992). *The schoolhome.* Cambridge, MA: Harvard University Press.

McManus, M. (1996, June 22). Schools teaching moral values see behavior, academic change. *The Canton Repository,* p. B4.

Meier, D. (2002). *The power of their ideas.* Boston: Beacon Press.

Mills, N. (1997). *The triumph of meanness.* Boston: Houghton, Mifflin.

Minnich, E. K. (2003, September/October). Teaching thinking: Moral and political considerations. *Change, 35*(5), 19–24.

Murdoch, I. (1970). *The sovereignty of good.* Boston: Routledge & Kegan Paul.

Noddings, N. (1984). *Caring: A feminine approach to ethics and moral education.* Berkeley: University of California Press.

Noddings, N. (1992). *The challenge to care in schools.* New York: Teachers College Press.

Noddings, N. (1999). Care, justice and equity. In M. S. Katz, N. Noddings, & K. A. Strike (Eds.), *Justice and caring: The search for common ground in education* (pp. 7–20). New York: Teachers College Press.

Noddings, N. (2002). *Educating moral people.* New York: Teachers College Press.

Orfield, G., Eaton, S., & Harvard Project on School Desegregation. (1996). *Dismantling desegregation: The quiet reversal of Brown v. Board of Ed.* New York: New Press.

Palincsar, A. S., & Brown, A. L. (1986). Interactive teaching to promote independent learning from text. *The Reading Teacher, 39,* 771–777.

Palmer, P. (1998). *The courage to teach.* San Francisco: Jossey-Bass.

Panichas, G. A. (Ed.). (1977). *Simone Weil reader.* Wakefield, RI: Moyer Bell.

Pappano, L. (2004, January 4). Offering aid to parents. *Boston Globe,* pp. E1, 7.

Parker, W. C. (Ed.). (1996). *Educating the democratic mind.* Albany: State University of New York Press.

Perry, W. (1981). Cognitive and ethical growth: The making of meaning. In A. W. Chickering (Ed.), *The modern American college* (pp. 76–116). San Francisco: Jossey-Bass.

Piaget, J. (1965). *The moral judgment of the child.* New York: Free Press. (Original work published 1932)

Piaget, J. (1979). *The child's conception of the world.* Totowa: NJ: Littlefield, Adams.

Plotz, J. (1999, November). Thinking out loud. *Lingua Franca Book Review, 9*(8), B43, 45.

Putnam, R. D. (2000). *Bowling alone: The collapse and revival of American community.* New York: Simon & Schuster.

Raider-Roth, M. (2005). *Trusting what you know.* San Francisco: Jossey-Bass.

Rawls, J. (1999). *A theory of justice.* Cambridge, MA: Harvard University Press.

Rich, A. C. (1978). *On lies, secrets, and silence: Selected prose 1966–1978.* New York: Norton.

Ruddick, S. (1989). *Maternal thinking: Towards a politics of peace.* Boston: Beacon Press.

Rury, J. L. (2002). *Education and social change.* Mahwah, NJ: Erlbaum.

Schrader, D. (1999). Justice and caring: Process in college students' moral reasoning development. In M. S. Katz, N. Noddings, & K. A. Strike (Eds.), *Justice and caring: The search for common ground in education* (pp. 37–59).

Secor, L. (2004, January 18). Measuring morals. *The Boston Globe*, pp. H1, H5.

Selman, R. (2003, December 1). The promotion of social awareness. An interview with Larsen Professor Robert Selman. HGSE News. www.gse.harvard.edu/news/features/selman/12012003.

Simmons, R. G. (1987, Fall). Social transition and adolescent development. In C. E. Irwin, Jr. (Ed.), *Adolescent social behavior and health* (pp. 33–61). San Francisco: Jossey-Bass.

Stansbury, R. (1997, March 4). Popular get-tough policies don't extend to cheating in schools. *The Hartford Courant Co*, pp. A1, A5.

Tannen, D. (1998). *The argument culture.* New York: Ballantine Books.

Tobin, K. (1991, April). *Multiple perspectives on teaching.* Paper presented at the annual meeting of the American Educational Research Association, Chicago.

Ulrich, L. T. (2000, June). Getting all the butter from a duck. Keynote address presented at *Women's private writing/writing women's history*, University of New England, Portland, ME.

Vygotsky, L. S. (1978). *Mind in society.* Cambridge, MA: Harvard University Press.

Walker, L. (1984). Sex differences in the development of moral reasoning: A critical review. *Child Development, 55,* 677–691.

Index

About the Auth

D. KAY JOHNSTON ⌐
Studies at Colgate Univers
as Chair of the Educational St⌐
Studies Program. She has also ta⌐
and recently spent three semesters
the Holy Cross. Before she earned ⌐
School of Education, she taught in publ⌐
chusetts. Her interests are in moral develc⌐
Her work has appeared in *The Journal of Mor*⌐
Record [on-line], *The Journal of Youth and Adole*⌐
well as in books about moral development and te⌐
coediting a book on the challenges and possibilities ⌐
at liberal arts institutions. She lives in Cambridge, Ma
Hamilton, New York.